contents

Drawings by:
Michele Roberts 43
Stef Pixner 7, 10, 12, 14, 19, 37, 41, 45, 50, 58, 61, 63.
Alison Fell 5, 54, 71, 73, 74, 75, 79, 86, 90, 93, 96, 100, 108, 124

Photographs by:
James Swinson 98, 99.

smile smile smile smile

Alison Fell
Stef Pixner
Tina Reid
Michele Roberts
Ann Oosthuizen

Sheba Feminist Publishers

Smile, smile, smile, smile was first published by Sheba
Feminist Publishers, 488 Kingsland Road, London E8 in
September, 1980
© the collection, Sheba Feminist Publishers
© individual work, the authors
ISBN 0 907179 03 7
Typeset in 10 and 11pt Theme by Dark Moon, 43 All Saints
Road, London W11
Cover design by An Dekker
Printed by A. Wheaton & Co. Ltd.., Exeter

STEF PIXNER

train and the river

riverrace swollen lace poisoned foam cold screaming
five o'clock whistle blowing your face like an old
blue eyed mountain craggy with straw beard running
along by the ice black flood river jumping
from sleeper to sleeper those huge chunks of grey
wood the iron rails quiet beside the surging
spring water and under the sleeping black train   a row
                                                  of peerless
                                                  icicles

mugshots: before and after

I

four sullen photographs
fall from the chute

my jaw says (four times)
"i hate you for going"

II

i see you wave
clear and small at the end
of the bridge between train and plane

there was scarlet paint
sharp sunlight
the ticket collector's cap

III

last week in the same booth
we kissed for the camera

now i hold our love
in a strip. four snaps

between two fingers
                    smile
                    smile
                    smile
                    smile

love poem

i love all the fat bits of you
and the hairy bits
and the smooth round silky masses of you
and the light inside you when you shine
and your serious obsessional mind
reaching out for the moon and totality
and your white legs in red slippers
and your clear eyes and your stories
and your dominance and your submission
and the feeling of your presence
and your warm arms
and you

the second toothbrush, is it hers?
or do you have two now
you brought mine back?

why is it the tooth
brush
that hurts
the worst?

choice: the cutting edge

I

there's a rock in my pocket
cuts a hole in my jacket

II

panic. the world's unsafe
my belly knows it.
better to sleep forever
without a charming
spellbreaker

III

alone
in the dry river
bed of my worst
fears she told me;
'pick up a stone'.

smooth and bald
safe as eggs
the rock of ages
nestled
perfect in my hands;
no finger hold
no crack
to let me in.

IV

i smashed it;
like a cup it cracked
on the stones.

the sharp pieces
cursed me,
their raw edges and
silver veins
glittered
angry as secrets

V

and i saw
blood
at the edge
of the flickering screen.

dogs, seagulls, umbrellas

every day i talk too much
it's my job
i get paid for it

at lunch
i go to a cafe near a park
i drink coffee, eat omellettes,
listen to other people talk

today i walked back through the park
the bare green grass
                    spread out wide as fish eye lens
the grey sky billowed

i saw dogs
        seagulls
        umbrellas

the seagulls cried out
                    and chased the dogs
the umbrellas burst out
                    like butterflies

a slice of lemon coloured light
opened up
            behind the high arching black trees
the skyline grew ominously crystal small

and then the rain came down

think lucky

I

sunset falls
like blood
on the clockface

smell
of pepper and pine
and fresh rain

II

he says
think lucky

i say
the world is outside
your will

and mine

III

(tho' we may
act
on it)

IV

for ten dollars
he sells his blood
wears out his shoes
looking for the lucky break

V

i feel panic
in downtown cafes

he sees
the fear rise
says run
we'll outwit
it

grabs my hand

we leave fear
behind
on Telegraph Hill

VI

Christmas chronicle:

the newspapers
reek of death

Shah's troops
kill mourning
masses
in Iran

thirty three dead
boys
found under
ranch house home, Chicago
(the smell
of excavation
is terrible)

Guyana:
900
cyanide suicides
terminate
such an excess
of hope

VII

he says
it's a lack of love
in the world

i say
perhaps

it boils down
to that

VIII

after a lot
of boiling

IX

sunset stains
the clock face

i think lucky
(just in case)

morning;
in my bowl
green light.
sky burns
turns through
blue silence.
every real sound
falls
on open ears.
i go down now
to the sea
without doubts.

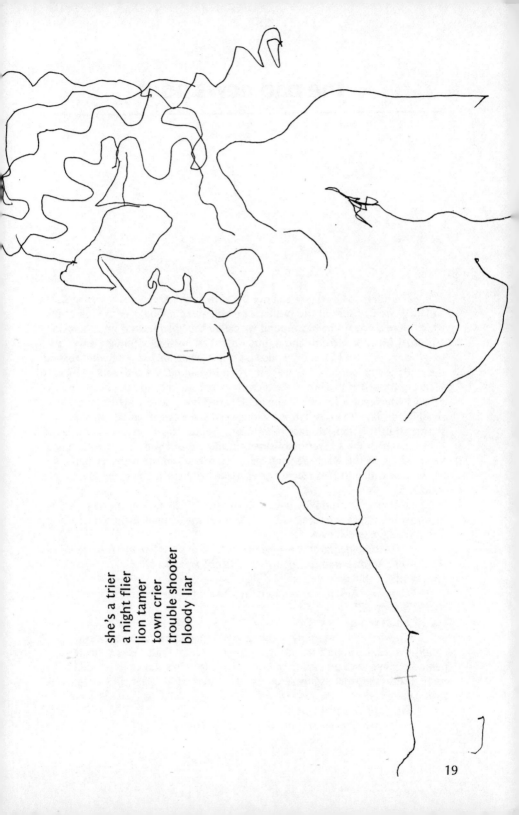

she's a trier
a night flier
lion tamer
town crier
trouble shooter
bloody liar

19

the bad news pool

The hill rose khaki green above us, with a dark crest of trees on it, bare and lacy. We had skirted the swell of the hill, and climbed over the tail of it which sloped down to a black pond we called the "bad news pool". It wasn't our usual way home from school, but Anita had insisted, although it was a long way round, and I usually ended up doing what she did. The wind rustled the reeds by the pond, a slithery, other-worldy sound. We had walked there in silence. I looked at my brown leather shoes as I walked, and the brave spikes of grass which stuck up out of the mud. It had been raining lightly but steadily for days. Once or twice I had looked sideways at Anita, but she was staring straight ahead, her face determined, her jaw tight. She had the kind of fine skin which shows every movement of muscle and bone under it. She had taken off her beret. Rain spangled her thick fringe and the wisps of light brown hair which fluffed round her ears like baby curls. She stopped suddenly.

"Come on, Anita. Why have you stopped?" She sat down on her brown cardboard schoolcase in the mud and stared at me triumphantly out of slightly bulging green eyes.

" 'The time has come,' the Walrus said, 'To talk of many things: Of shoes — and ships — and sealing-wax — Of cabbages and kings —'." It was raining still, a thin grey determined rain.

"Come on Anita" I said miserably. "We'll be late home."

"So what?"

"Mum will be cross."

"So what? . . . 'Mummy will be cross' " she repeated in a mocking childish voice. I couldn't think of anything to say to that. Tears collected behind my eyes and pressed hard into the sockets, like knuckles pressed in there. I didn't let them squeeze out. I stared back at her. Her eyes were a very light clear green.

"Why are you sitting down, Anita?"

" 'The time has come,' the Walrus said, 'To talk of many things' " she repeated in an oily, wheedling voice, with a threat running softly under it. She took off her navy gaberdine schoolcoat, folded it and put it down on the sodden grass. She loosened the schooltie at her throat.

"Oh Anita, come on. You'll get soaked."

"I don't mind. I like the rain. Don't you Hetty? I thought you liked the rain? 'The time has come, the Walrus said' —"

"Stop it!"

"Stop it!" she mimicked, sitting on the edge of her case, the rain beginning to blotch and darken her school jumper. The sky sagged round us, shutting us in. It was hard to believe it was the same place we had come to last summer, the day we hopped off school.

Then, the sky had expanded. The hill rolled green and easy, with grasses which rippled at the tips, and tall white umbrella flowers. Anita lived without a father like I did, and soon after we left for schools every day, our mothers left for work. That day, we hid in some bushes, and I got out a box of paints I'd hidden in my satchel. I painted a black moustache under Anita's turned up nose, and lines up the back of her legs, like stocking seams. She painted me a beauty spot, and a black eye in bruise colours, mottled purple and blue. We waded in the mud by the stream; it was orange as tomato soup. Her bare legs were marked with the painted on stocking seams, and the splashes of bright mud.

We bought a big sheet of paper, took it home, and laid it on the floor. Anita painted one side, and I painted the other. We called the finished painting "The beginning of the world". It was bursting with trees and waterfalls, flowers and animals, but no human beings. There were mountain peaks in the far distance lit up by a gory sunset. I pinned the picture to my wall and looked at it at night in bed. I imagined running over the round green hills, and putting my face in the bright water.

"Don't imitate me!"

"Don't imitate me!" she echoed, smiling up at me, her wet pink cheeks and green eyes the brightest colour in the four o'clock rainy winter twilight. She pulled her jumper off and threw it down.

"Ah, that's better" she said with satisfaction. "Aren't you hot?" She never wore scarf or gloves even when it snowed. Even when she was ill in bed she threw the covers off. She believed in the absolute power of will; if she willed it hard enough, the elements could do her no harm. Her hands, gripping the case on either side of her body so the knuckles showed white, were raw and cracked.

"It's because of all the scrubbing I have to do" she once said, looking at me as if I never did anything. I didn't do very much, it was true. I dried the dishes and cleaned out the mice Anita's mother had brought home for me from the research laboratory where she worked. Her mother was hard on Anita when she came home from work, if the housework hadn't been done. Anita had to look after her little brother, too. He was pale and difficult, with the pointed chin of a cherub. He didn't have to do any housework. He was spoiled and told tales. Anita led him a dance when her mother was out, and he kicked her in return.

Her father visited on Sundays. Then they had a big fire in the grate, and cake hot from the oven with butter. I often went round on Sunday afternoons. Anita's mother sat in a painted wooden armchair wearing the jewellery her ex-husband had made her. The cats sat round the fire with them. Anita and I lay stretched out on the floor, playing. It was a lofty white room, with firelight leaping on the walls, full of the sound of comfortable laughter.

"Look at the little man, sitting on that log" said Anita.

"Where?"

"Over there, look. He's got red and white striped socks, and he's fishing. Can't you see him?" I took off my glasses, and wiped them free of rain. All I could see was the small silhouette of a man on top of the hill against the low bellied clouds.

"No."

"*You* can't see *anything.*"

"I can. There's nobody there."

"You only say that because you can't see him."

"I can see him. He's not there. Come on Anita, come home."

"Come on Anita" she mocked.

"*Damn* you!" I said. It was my strongest language. Before she had time to echo and ridicule my rage, I pushed her chest and she fell over backwards in the mud. She lay there with her eyes shut and a beatific expression on her face, spreadeagled in the muddy grass, the rain beating down on her chest through her thin school shirt.

"This rain is wonderful" she said. I wanted to trample all over her, kick her till her superior face cracked. Instead I crouched down. I scooped up some cold mud in my fingers and stood over her. I dropped some on her chest, and the rest on her peaceful, saint-like face. I began to feel a little better.

" 'The time has come,' the Walrus said, 'To talk' . . ."

"All right, so you want to talk. Go on then. What d'you want to say?"

"Isn't it obvious? Can't you guess? I don't want to be your friend any more. Brenda and Val don't either. We think you're a show off. And I don't want to walk home from school with you any more, either."

The rain thinned to a drizzle, and a patch of clouds turned to silver above the reeds and willows. A flock of seagulls wintering inland circled nearby, whirling like ash from a fire, before they settled. A crow flapped towards a wooden post and perched there, waiting. The man was no longer silhouetted. He had come down off the crown of the hill and was slowly walking in our direction. I crouched down again and scooped up some mud. I smeared it on my face. It was soft and very cold. I felt some relief. Anita still lay stretched out on the ground. I set off towards the rim of the hill. Every footstep squelched. The rain had begun to penetrate my shoes, and dribble down the back of my neck. The wildness of the sky gave a certain comfort. About halfway up the hill, I passed the man coming down it. I couldn't see much of his face. He had his coat collar turned up, and a hat pulled down to keep the rain off. I looked back, although I'd promised myself I wouldn't. Anita was still lying there, face to the sky. From that height the pond had taken on the silver grey of the sky, and the brown of the bare willows round it. I went on. Near the top of the hill, I couldn't stop myself from looking back once again.

When I turned round I couldn't see Anita any more, I could only see the man, lying face down where she had been lying. I heard a sound which could have been a human scream, or a seagull's cry. I wiped my glasses again. Then I saw Anita's legs flailing from underneath the man's black coat. I dropped my satchel and ran down the long khaki green slope of the hill, jumping over tussocks of grass, slithering each time I landed. The gulls flew above my head with their watery cries. The man half sat up on his knees. He was still on top of Anita, but he was undoing his trouser buttons with one hand, and one of her arms was now free. Suddenly the rain lashed down. There was a massive hissing and pattering sound. It got very dark. The rain was vertical and thick. The seagulls settled and stopped their crying. As I ran towards them I had no plan in mind. I had no mind; I was only a pair of legs running, a moving thing on the hill. Rain streamed down my glasses. I slowed down and pulled them off. The man ahead was now only a dark blur; Anita, a paler one, was visible to me only because I already knew she was there. When I reached them, I put my glasses back on again.

The man hadn't heard me; he didn't look round. Anita saw me come up behind him. I grabbed the collar of his heavy coat and pulled him backwards. He was surprised and toppled more easily than I expected, onto his back. Anita leapt up. Her face was squeezed tight as if she was having a tantrum. She looked like her little brother for a moment as she stood on one leg and brought the other foot hard down into the dark crutch of the man's trousers. He cried out and curled up instantly into a ball, like a woodlouse when its protective stone is taken away. We ran off up the hill, leaving Anita's cardboard schoolcase, her coat and her jumper, lying next to him in the mud. At the top of the hill I made a detour to pick up my satchel.

"*Come on Hetty!*" Anita shouted hoarsely through the rain.

"It's got all my homework in it!" I shouted back. I ran after her, my satchel flapping.

everybody loves saturday night

I liked the sight of blood.

"It's like a red smile" I said to the nurse. She didn't laugh, but sewed up up the crescent shaped gash with black thread. After all, it was gone 11 p.m.

"Now it's got black teeth." I looked up for her smile, but there was none.

*

A man of words, and not of deeds
Is like a garden full of weeds
And when the weeds begin to grow
It's like a garden full of snow

It was one of my favourite poems.

"Morbid child" my mother laughed when I chanted:

And when the wall begins to crack
It's like a stick across your back
And when your back begins to bleed
O then you're dead and dead indeed.

*

"You'll be scarred for life" she said.
"I don't care. It doesn't bother me."
"You're not going out for 3 months, my girl."
"Oh Mum . . ."

*

There in the bloody crimson pool
Drowns the bloody crimson fool
Floundering on the moonshot rocks
Are broken brains like broken crocks
Broken bodies in a building heap
While pretty maids and children weep

"I've written a poem Mum. Do you like it?"
"It's rather gloomy, Deborah. Too much blood in it for me."

*

"IF I WERE TICKLED BY THE RUB OF LOVE" he growled, he thundered. I lay back on his divan. I was rigid. His hair stuck up like a brush from his smooth white forehead. His lion's voice surged in the room:

A rooking girl who stole me for her side
Broke through her straws, breaking my bandaged string

White moon face and humble, greedy smile. We each bore our emblems. My bandage, wound round my right calf. It bulged white under my black stocking. ("Black stockings" she laughed. "Had to wear them when I was at school. Horrible things." In the streets people stared and I looked straight ahead. "Dirty beatnik" was what they wanted to say.) His bandage, wound round his left foot, bulky under his grey nylon sock.

"Tell me what you think of this." Sasha faced me. He balanced a record carefully between his square white forefingers. He had his very own record player. At home we had one in the kitchen for all of us. I examined the writing on the sleeve; the record was called "The Rite of Spring". Suddenly unfamiliar sounds bounced round me. They wouldn't stop long enough for me to hear, let alone think anything about them.

"It's like fireworks exploding" I said, hopefully. Sasha looked pleased with my answer. He watched me for a while as if I was a rare natural object he had come across unexpectedly on a country walk. He looked happy.

"Do you like looking at photographs?" He placed a dark red leather bound album in my lap. The music spluttered about my ears. I turned the stiff brown pages. Delicate white paper separated each leaf. There were naked bodies on almost every page. The music shrieked. White bodies, sepia tinted, set against rocks, olive groves, sandy beaches. His family went abroad for their holidays and took their clothes off when they got there. I wouldn't even let my family in the bathroom. No lock on the door, so I had to shout "Go away! I'm in here!" My brother barged in once. "You take so long," he complained. There was always a lot to think about in the bathroom. The cream paint peeling above the bath which stood on lion's paws. The dust

25

under it, and the flowing green stain from the tap to the plughole. The contents of the cupboard from which I tried to piece together the details of my mother's intimate life. The texture of the skin on my knees. New hair appearing in private places, strong and curly. *"Hurry up!"* he called. Had I ever seen him with nothing on? No picture came to mind. But there was my mother's body, veiled by a ghostly blue nightdress, like someone who has drowned. I turned the pages quickly, so as not to seem too interested. There in front of me, page after page. Big penises and small ones. All kinds of breasts.

Their sexual emblems hung nonchalantly from the bodies of Sasha, his mother, father, and an assortment of friends. They reclined in deckchairs, drank wine, laughed, ate grapes. I was turning the pages too fast to see properly. I longed to be alone with the album and a magnifying glass. Once or twice I dared to put my face close to the page, but I couldn't quite see what I wanted. I didn't know exactly what I wanted to see. Photographs are elusive, like mirrors; you can't see behind them. I flicked the pages. The music banged and crashed. Sasha looked over my shoulder, his chin hovering a fraction above it.

"That one's nice. Looks a nice place. Who's that?" I searched for appropriate things to say. I didn't know what was appropriate.

"Where's your toilet?" I escaped up the broad stairs, across the black and white tiled hall. It was a large room for a lavatory. The walls were hung with painted ladies, huge, colourful, naked, relaxed. There were joke postcards pinned to the door. I didn't get many of the jokes. I was so nervous I had to wait a long time to pee. Beyond the high ceilinged W.C. was the grand house that smelt of polish and spices, books, and another smell, like the smell of boarding houses and cream teas.

Sasha's family occupied the entire house in what was known amongst my friends as "millionaire's row". His parents bought it years ago, when property was cheap, soon after they fled from Germany in the thirties. His grandparents were killed by the Nazis. I thought it was wrong to live off rent from lodgers. Sasha said they were very cheap rooms, and it was better to have his parents as landlords, than some others. The front of the house was imposing. I felt sick when I pressed the front door bell; I hoped wildly that he'd forgotten our arrangement and gone out. I waited a couple of seconds, and was ready to run to freedom down the front steps, when I saw his shape through the intricate coloured glass, moving towards me across the wide hall.

*

All men are false says my mother
They'll tell you wicked loving lies
The very next evening they'll court another
Leave you alone to pine and sigh

I sang on my way to school, those mornings when I was in a good mood.

Another favourite was: "It ain't no sin, to take off your skin, and dance around in your bones." "I don't think that is suitable for a girl of your age." "What's rude about it Mum?" I was genuinely puzzled. She didn't explain. She had a pile of old 78 records. The Red Army singing "Kulinka" and "The Internationale" and strange music from Greece, Armenia, Uzbekistan. I loved that music. Listened to it leaning out of the kitchen window. There I was, a little girl with plaits among the birch trees and snow of the Urals. There were my Ukrainian ancestors, with fur hats and embroidered blouses, and my grandfather, a handsome fiery young man, fleeing a pogrom in his shirt sleeves, escaping on a sledge through the snow. Sound of the sleigh bells. Volga boatmen. Pushkin dying in a duel. Our Lenin.

"Don't be silly. Your ancestors didn't wear embroidered peasant clothes. Your great grandfather was a rabbi. He wore black."

*

"Do you like Dylan Thomas?" Sasha asked me, picking up a volume of his "Collected Poems".

"He's all right" I said. I'd never read any Dylan Thomas, though I'd heard the name.

> *Shall it be male or female? say the fingers*
> *That chalk the walls with green girls and their men.*
> *I would not fear the muscling in of love*
> *If I were tickled by the urchin hungers*
> *Rehearsing heat upon a raw-edged nerve.*

*

At school I wore grey uniform and worried that really I was a man. Amongst the hundreds of girls I stalked, an imposter, with my solid jawline, severe forehead, and lace up shoes. At night I ran my fingers over my silky skin. "I'll remember this when I'm middle aged and don't have silky skin any more." We had no curtains and the light from the street threw window patterns on to the brown fernlike wallpaper. They swung across the ceiling as cars passed in the street below. My toes avoided the cold areas of the bed. My toes, the cars. Me, the street, London, England, the world. The sky, the milky way. My toes, toe nails, skin, cells; subatomic particles, zooming through space like stars in the universe. "What's beyond the sky Mummy?" I asked when I was small. "Nothing lies beyond the sky. It just goes on and on." That was difficult to think about. The world was easier, tho' it was in such a mess. If only they would ask me! Maybe since they can't agree on anything they will decide to put the fate of the world in the hands of one person. They will draw lots. Firstly, which country, out of all the countries in the world? By chance, it will be England. Which part of England? London. Which age? Fourteen. Which school? Guy Fawkes Hill. Which class? 4H. Which sex?

Female. Which girl? Me of course. I will tell them to share it all out equally. "We'll make Sir Winston Churchill smoke a Woodbine every day." It was all so obvious.

*

Suddenly I surveyed the party through a jagged hole. I don't remember the sound of breaking glass. I didn't even push the window very hard. We had been playing a silly game with a rose in a milkbottle. The boys passed it from hand to hand, the girls tried to get it from them. The boys were tall, smug and teasing. I played to win. When I caught the dark red rose, I tried to look demure; I tried to hide my triumphant smile.

As I ran, one of the boys opened the french windows and shoved me out into the November mud. I pushed on the window. Suddenly I saw the party through a jagged hole. Someone pointed to my leg. I looked down, at the black and the red. Black stocking, red crescent of blood. It went with my outfit; a red and black checked mohair skirt, and a black jumper. Someone dialled 999. People gathered round and asked me how I was. I began to feel at home in the party.

"Hallo. What happened to you?" Sasha was already sitting in the ambulance when I got into it. He was wearing one black shoe. I wore one black stocking. "I was on the other side of the window" he said. "I didn't know that you were hurt too." A fragment of glass had pierced the tongue of his shoe, and punctured an artery. I'd never been in an ambulance before. Dark streets flashed by. To think, I nearly hadn't come. I had planned to spend the evening at home with Joan, but she wanted to go to the party.

"We haven't been invited."

"It doesn't matter, everybody does it." Maybe tonight. Maybe tonight I'll see him. He'll come over to me as I stand shyly in a dark corner, and strike up a conversation. He'll be wearing jeans and suede shoes. He'll sit down beside me and play the guitar. He won't mind my awkwardness. He'll want to see me again.

"What's your name?" asked Sasha. He didn't know me. He hadn't crashed the party. He knew the crowd.

*

"Do you masturbate?" he asked. Sasha sat next to me on the divan. The room shook with the Rites of Spring. "Now I want you to be frank with me . . ." Ghosts from Uzbekistan. Girls with 12 pigtails and embroidered headbands, mountainous dreamers from Georgia wandering the road to Samarkand. Pushkin's witch, flying through the night in her pestle and mortar to visit a house which runs on hen's legs. Animal spirits from Sierra Leone, Hans Andersen's mermaid, lying on the beach in her grief, struck dumb for love. Many things I knew from sitting at my mother's side.

I said nothing. Sasha was smaller than I, next to me on the divan. His trousers were too short. His body too round. He stood up and put some jazz on the record player. Strange sounds to me. No tune or words. It was boring. Thelonius Monk, John Coltrane. I didn't catch the names that afternoon; I learned them later. Later, when I hung around with the cool cats who smoked weed and charge on Friday and Saturday nights when we had no homework.

"Listen to that riff, man." What riff? What was a riff? How did you find out what a riff was? I listened hard and kept quiet until in the end I heard something too. The saxophone separate from the piano, from the bass guitar. The blue notes. Eventually with money from my Saturday morning job, I bought my own jazz records, Charlie Mingus, Miles Davis, Charlie Bird.

I had said nothing. I wish he was goodlooking; I wish I liked him. Instead I feel sorry for him. But perhaps I can grow to like him? It must be obvious to him that I don't understand. I know that the question, like the poetry, has something to do with sex. I know it by the special way he asks me; studiously honest, scientific. Sasha is not prudish. He is like Dylan Thomas, full of lust and life. I'm flattered to be asked such an adult question; to have been singled out, chosen.

"You know, do you touch yourself, your breasts, your body?" His forehead is shiny and his trousers are too short. I don't want to be prudish. I want to pass the honesty test. I'm sensible; I don't blink or blush or giggle. But something else is lurking behind those protruding ears. "If I were tickled by the rub of love." Rub, roar, rasp. Rasp, clasp, grasp. Rub, rubbing, roaring, rasping, grasping, gasping. Oh. At night I hold my breasts, I run my hands along my skin, admiring its smoothness, imagining someone else admiring it, running their hands over it where only I have touched, under the sheets. I look up, look him straight in the eyes.

"Yes" I answer. I am very brave.

*

"Hallo Mum . . . sorry I wasn't back by 11. I'm at St. Joseph's Hospital. Don't worry, it's nothing serious, I just cut my leg and I've had a few stitches. You don't have to come and collect me, I can walk back with Sasha . . ."

"What do you mean, I don't have to collect you! Of course I'm coming to collect you! What have you been doing? My God . . . Who is this Sasha? I've got a few words to say to him."

"See you soon then Mum. I'll need another coat, I left mine behind at the party — but *please* don't bring my schoolcoat!" I handed the 'phone to Sasha. My mother's voice resounded in the telephone booth.

"Everything's all right Mrs. Poliakoff" he tried to reassure her in his pompous schoolboy tones. I couldn't hear her replies, only the sharpness in her voice, which was getting higher and higher. He put the receiver to my ear. "What do you mean by this behaviour? My child is only fourteen . . ." After some minutes

"DON'T BE SO BUMPTIOUS!" he roared, and slammed the phone

down.

We sat and waited on a wooden bench in the hospital foyer. Nurses bustled past us. I felt sick. She would be so worried and angry. A moment later I smiled at the memory of Sasha's impeccably cultured voice, booming out like a foghorn, "Don't be so *bumptious!*"

"I would like to meet you again" he said. "Why don't you come round next Saturday afternoon?" I paused. I can't say no. How can I say no? He will look so hurt. I will have to think of an excuse very quickly. And it's nice to be asked out. He's older than me. He's obviously clever and interesting and knows more people than I do. Maybe he finds me attractive? I might find I like him after all. First impressions can be deceptive. Go on, give it a try.

"Yes, Sasha" I said. But my heart wasn't in it.

Just then, my mother arrived carrying my schoolcoat bundled under her arm.

*

The record was over and he had finished reading. The room was very quiet. Outside the wide Victorian windows blue tits hopped on the branches of a twisted hawthorn tree. Pale sun fell on the white paint of the built-in cupboard, the bookshelves, the remains of our Saturday afternoon tea. He looked at me intimately.

"Do *you* write poetry?" he asked.

> *And there she sat — like cold grey stone*
> *Pale as dead, alone —*
> *The news . . . it pierced her like the keenest blade*
> *Her hair fell still, her eyes were glazed*
> *Her hands of chillest ice were made . . .*

I wrote poems all the time. Tragedies, cautionary tales, political verse. I had written 2 since we met in the ambulance. I was proud of them. I thought I'd grown up a lot in the last week.

> *Everybody loves Saturday night*
> *A party folks, burnsville, let's go*
> *Nobody enjoys parties*
> *'Hallo! hallo! hallo! hallo!'*

Poetry. Sasha smiled at me encouragingly. A tender, gaptoothed, patronizing smile. Poetry. Mum said the Bible was full of it. "Awake, awake, Deborah; awake, awake; utter a song . . . Blessed among women shall Jael the wife of Heber the Kenite be; blessed shall she be above women in the tent. He asked for water, and she gave him milk; she brought forth butter in a lordly dish. She put her hand to the nail, and her right hand to the workman's hammer; and with the hammer she smote Sisera, she smote off his head. When she had pierced and stricken through his temples at her feet he bowed, he fell, he lay down: at her feet he bowed, he fell: where he bowed, there he fell down dead . . . So let all thine enemies perish, O Lord."

She said I could choose: I could go to Jewish or Christian teaching and prayers or opt out of school religion altogether. I didn't believe in God, but I wanted to read the Bible, that treasure house of ancient songs and tales. "All the rivers run into the sea; yet the sea is not full; unto the place from whence the rivers come, thither they return again. All things are full of labour; man cannot utter it: the eye is not satisfied with seeing, nor the ear filled with hearing . . . For in much wisdom is much grief: and he that increaseth knowledge increaseth sorrow." She read aloud to me as I dried my long hair in front of the fire on Saturday evenings. Was that true, about wisdom and sorrow? I watched the fiery palaces crumble in the grate, and the green flames that burst out from the coal.

Poetry. Miss Peppermartin didn't wear a bra and showered the girls in the front row with her spit. Keats and Shelley. Her face lit up like a child's. Her head was sunk into her shoulders, but her hands were up in the air, her eyes on some vision of her own, like a small girl inside an old skin, a small girl with frizzy hair, in love with poetry. She encouraged us to write.

> *If only I could create*
> *In a world of destruction!*
> *Put meaning*
> *Into this meangingless world*
>
> *Where everyone acts*
> *And where values are false*
>
> *In a fluid blue world*
> *I want to hold on to something*
> *Someone*
> *Someone I know is solid.*
> *But the people,*
> *Boys, I know*
> *I cannot trust, no*

Sasha was looking at me, waiting for me to say something. I had the poems with me, in a blue exercise book in my duffle bag.

> *Because they don't mean what they say*
> *And the kisses*
> *And the embraces*
> *Mean nothing*
> *Anymore.*

31

It is a world of space.
Beneath us the waters
Of fear
Flow ceaselessly —
Beneath the piles
On which we build our lives
Like Amsterdam . . .

The waistband of my mohair skirt cut in to my stomach.
    "Tomorrow I'll go on a diet." Sasha needs to go on a diet too; he has a round belly. Sasha lacks style. He doesn't know what to wear or how to wear it.

The sun pools its golden light
And my flesh is firm
And brown
And solid.

Do not let me wander
Alone.

I cannot be
Alone
While I am in the world.

I lacked style too. He said my silver pendant would look better when parts of the silver had gone black. It was too gaudy. He fingered the pendant, as it hung on my chest. Wide white fingers, so near to my breasts. I panicked.
    "No." I said. "I don't write poetry . . . I'd better be going now, Mum will be expecting me back. I can't stay out late, after last Saturday."
    "But you said she wasn't coming home till 9 o'clock this evening. I thought we were going to walk together to Tony's party? What's come over you Deborah? I know — you're frightened of me. Don't be frightened of me, I don't want to hurt you, I never want to hurt you." My mouth opened, but no sound came out. I knew what it was like to feel gauche and clumsy. To laugh too loud, to be too serious, to have breasts that are too large and ankles too thick, front teeth too big, hair too straight, and cheeks too fat and rosy.
    "It must be terrible, to feel you're not physically attractive to the opposite sex" I thought out loud. It was a big mistake.
    "I often do" he said. His eyes were grateful. He smiled hopefully, a mischievous, greedy, gaptoothed smile. I looked down at his polished black shoes. "If I were tickled by the rub of love." That's when I should have left. The photograph album. Every page I turned was like accepting the invitation in his roaring voice. I should have closed the album. Banged it shut. Too bad that I wanted to look at the naked bodies, too bad if Sasha thought I was an ungenerous and frigid girl, on the side of narrow convention. I should have

said "Sasha, I'm not feeling well, I have to go" or "Sasha, I don't like you in *that kind of way*; let's just be friends." I should say it now . . . My mouth opened, but no sound came out.

*

"Don't be ashamed of your natural feelings, Debby." No sounds in the darkness except for Joan's younger sisters' breathing, and the tick of the alarm clock. Inside the sleeping bag, I slipped my hands under the flannel nightie. It smelled faintly of her. I cupped my hands round my heavy breasts.

"I've got a copy of Lady Chatterley's lover" whispered Joan. "My uncle gave it to me." Her uncle talked to her about sex; he told her about his affairs. Then she told me about them. Joan rustled the bedclothes and blew her nose.

Eggs and sperms and embryos. Funny feelings low in my belly. The heart which beat between my thighs for the first time two years ago, when John of Gaunt at last embraced Katheryn and made her his mistress.

"What's a wehorry?" I had asked my brother.

"Oh, a whore!" he laughed. "It's a bad woman; a woman who goes with men. What have you been reading? I think that book's too old for you."

"And what's *voluptuous*?"

"Oh . . . you'd say look at that voluptuous blonde over there."

"Yes, but what does it *mean*?"

"Look it up in the dictionary." I did. "Of or tending to sensuality." I looked up "Sensuality". That didn't help either.

I was seven when he commanded me to watch at the door for Mum, while he bore down on Marion, fighting and kicking on the bed. "Promise you'll never tell anybody." Their hair tangled together on the pillow. I kept watch, and kept my promise. "A boy can't help his sexual feelings, but he must learn to control them" Mum taught us. The feelings sweep over him, pulling down the corners of his eyes and his mouth. Then you are powerful if you can refuse him; you are all powerful, as long as you feel nothing. I lay in the dark and it occurred to me that all the fragments were connected by a central mystery I had not yet penetrated.

"Tomorrow I'm going to the Family Planning clinic with Sean's sister. She's married. You have to say you're married. I've borrowed a ring." Joan's voice was soft and conspiratorial. We were bound together by the darkness and our whispers. I basked in it. Joan was 2 years older than I was. She had broad shoulders and green eyes. "The important thing is to make an impression on people. It doesn't matter whether it's a good or a bad impression." Her nose wrinkled up when she laughed, and the laugh came out somewhere between a cackle and a snort.

"I'm going to spend a weekend with Sean while his parents are away. Do you think I should?"

"Answer me honestly, Deborah: what were your first impressions of me?" Sasha at the party. A short pale boy with a big voice, expounding in the corner.

"Camus writes better novels than Sartre; *he* should stick to philosophy."

"I thought you were a bloody show off . . . and that you state your opinions as if they are facts."

"You're so right, it's quite touching." Say no. Say it now. Say "Sasha, I'm afraid you don't understand. And what's more you have no right to force me into this corner." It was getting dark. He switched on the soft light next to his bed, and put on some mellow sounding jazz.

"Girls usually only like me as a companion, they're not interested in me as a lover. It's so wonderful that you're different. You're beautiful."

"I'm *not*."

"You look so pensive, so sad." His face begged me. I hadn't the heart to remove the unconfident white hand that crept over my knee.

He pushed me gently backwards onto the divan and stroked the hair off my forehead, the hair I had so carefully combed down to hide my spots and scabs. I noticed that my hands and feet were cold, and I wasn't comfortable. Say no, say no. His mouth has gone limp now, his eyes are drawn down. His forehead is creased like an old man's, but his cheeks are downy as a schoolboy's. Say no, say no. One moment slides into the next. I'll say no at the last minute. But he moves his hand gingerly from my forehead over the contours of my face to the large shapes of my breasts. He leans his square body over mine, his white moonface tortured with concentration. Suddenly that heart begins to beat between my legs. Say no, say no. Break away, fling him off. I don't have to explain myself, I don't have to look at his shattered face as I pick up my duffle coat and walk out of the door.

But my belly has begun to move, in and out, up and down. There are hearts beating all over me now, and I shut my eyes, so that I don't see him any more, up there above me. The hearts beat faster and faster, and I want it to happen, whatever it is, the mystery and the sly talk, and the jokes that I don't understand. I don't care any more, whether he is good looking, or whether I like him. He fumbles to undo my stout cotton brassiere. I raise myself on my elbows, unhook it and fling it across the room. I pull off my knickers and roll up my skirt. I know where to fumble, what to reach for, what to unhook.

I liked the sight of blood. I laughed when I saw the red on the sheets. So that was it. If I were tickled. The Uzbeki girls twirled and their plaits spun round with them, under an Asian sun. Mary Kingsley struggled through a Malayan swamp in her long skirts, never letting go of her Victorian umbrella.

"You make me feel so tender — you are precious. I never want to hurt you." I had almost forgotten him. Slowly I gathered up my clothes.

"I don't want to see you again, Sasha."

"But why, Deborah, why, why?"

"I just don't, that's all."

"You've taken the wrong decision."

"No, I don't think so."

"Deborah, you are like a shut door ... and I thought you were going to be so frank. Why does it always have to end like this?" I could think of an answer but I said nothing. My eyes were on the door.

"Let my last moment be happy." I gave him a clockwork kiss and a smile.

"Girls hold all the strings" he said bitterly as he walked with me down the wide hall.past the faces in dark frames to the front door.

*

Six months later I saw him again. 'TOO MUCH ARMOUR, TOO LITTLE BRAIN'; he carried a placard with a grey green painting of a dinosaur on it. I was carrying one that said 'FOUR MINUTES TO SUICIDE' in luminous pink letters. He smiled at me every time I caught his eye across the cold field. I smiled back at him till my cheeks ached. The march began to move out of the field towards the nuclear power station. I lost sight of the bobbing dinosaur. It began to drizzle. The crowd started singing "Don't you hear the H bombs thunder/Echo like the crack of doom?" I got out my plastic mac. The column stretched ahead. Joan had dyed her hair blonde for the occasion. She wore white lipstick and black lines round her green eyes. I joined in the singing; I knew all the words off by heart. Even Hans Anderson's mermaid opened her mouth and sang.

MICHELE ROBERTS

the amazon's song

I bruise myself on him
the rock man, parched, reserves
himself in case of further drought
he remembers ancient storms
he is fragile and he may break
my tears erode his base, my
blood spatters a fastidious peak

I burn myself on him
the ice man, far away, preserves
rich gardens under snow
and memories of mummy, her enormous lap
my heat drives wedges
to his anxious skin, my clumsy feet
precipitate an avalanche

I starve myself on him
the skinny man deserves
no less than this: I have become
harpy, snatching in the night
I have become wind, tempestuous
tossing, a home-brewed hurricane

I have cut off both breasts
and I will not
no, I will not

the vicar's wife's song

only Christ is my lover
whom I forgive
much: my misery, his silence; my
beauty is all for him, I shut
hooded eyes, my pale face
haggard
jerks with ecstasy and with irritation
at a filthy oven, at the eucharist

I bawl from wall to wall
my curiosity and my tense endearments
the tiny cardboard house
boxes my lust as dues for Holy Week

I should have been born
in the time of Teresa
or Joan, I want
splendour and style
I am ashamed of that

meanwhile, my husband, the clergyman
smoothes his hair in a separate room

he dons gold drag and smooches with God
I bully Jesus, I have
no peace

the mistresses' song to husbands

together two
cities tremble
        between
dark and glitter
bounding tensions pulse
            our
filthy hands sustain
your lace
      and prick
          your
newly-laundered smile for
wife
      whose boulevard of green
and iron frills you
tread for sunday pleasure
              we
your rich and necessary closet
mulch your oratory where nuns
as blue as sugar-bags ferment
the slum with prayer
            flesh
boxed in spikes our hungry gut
strings twist against your
mouth
which tastes
our cargo grown
in backyard
colonies

nightshift

up there
men and gods collide
down here
the night is black
with stars
        Orion
the Warrior
straddles the street

I drag my dirty linen
between his legs
into the space-age
launderette
nowhere to sit
               our
heads and legs
bow to the heat and wet
mouths busy
rinsing experience

my neighbour
stuffs a hundred
pairs of underpants
into the colour telly gone mad
kicks the door shut: ain't you
finished yet? come
on man, machine, ain't got
no time to waste

a final shudder
the white foam
spurts to the drain

later I lie
between your legs
upon clean linen
my laughter stains your white night

lady-novelist
limbering up after writing
her diary-

civilisation's acrobat

you insist
there are obsolescences:
hands that once curved over clumsy tools
carve chips in silicone, compute and clock
brain galaxies, cosmos of nerves and blood

soon, you sparkle
language will wither away
like wings on fish, binary counts
become collectors' items
like masculine-feminine, couples
and jealousy, we'll throw
new switches in the unconscious
and polka to the dialectic
of the paranormal

oh but you stir me up
you curvet in a colt's entrechats
whirl to my arms like
seeds that september scatters
fall, thudding like fruit
onto my earth, albeit
wishing to renounce
custom and gravity

civilization's acrobat
I dare you to include
these atavistic surges of mine
these sarabandes of the woman corsair
this centuries-old
collapse and cry

norfolk weekend

we swallow the air like earth
the sky is a delicate wall
on which we paint with clouds

the orchard stoops and drops
dark pink
apples in the long
grass, little
fallen sunsets in
green twilight

the land is pegged
with churches, five
on the horizon
but it still flaps brown
and stony

far across the field
the blackbirds chatter on
and red barns hug the earth
trees whistle for fled blue

blue tiles, blue roof, blue
dark sky

my grandmother is dying

death dons an apron
death stirs the pudding
death lets you lick the spoon

death rocks you
when you wake from nightmares
crooning: there, there, baby
don't cry

death takes your gifts
and props them on the mantel
death spoils you, death
dresses you in paper skirts
for Christmas pantomimes

death has wept so long, so often
death's breasts are withered
death takes medicine, death is bitchy
death laughs, death dances
hola death

death sits alone
and stares at darkness
death remembers
death is not polite, she burps and gossips
death says: God
gives with one hand
and with both hands
takes away

death, teach me your songs, your stories
let me hug your wisdom
one last time
death embrace me, death sit next to me

death oh my loved one my grandmother

red-haired lover

only your hair is on fire
beech forest tucked
under my chin's hill

blue midnight blankets you
curled small in my skin's cave
white reed of flesh
pale lily of juice

you spill your secrets' seed
all night
you grow me:
a giant mama-gourd

sometimes your red sun
rises in me

semi-detached wound

the spring is unbearable
the wet sun spatters
the smashed
house of the snail
and the hyacinth hurts and hurts

the birth of brawny weeds
their riotous assembly
rips apart
my pavement skin
that lovers tango on

oh my mouth
aching
and bruised by light
my eyelids
violent as plane leaves
in the dark rain

my waist
bends and bends

sap oozes, rises, bursts
in me
and runs
fresh hollowing tears

I holler at the moon

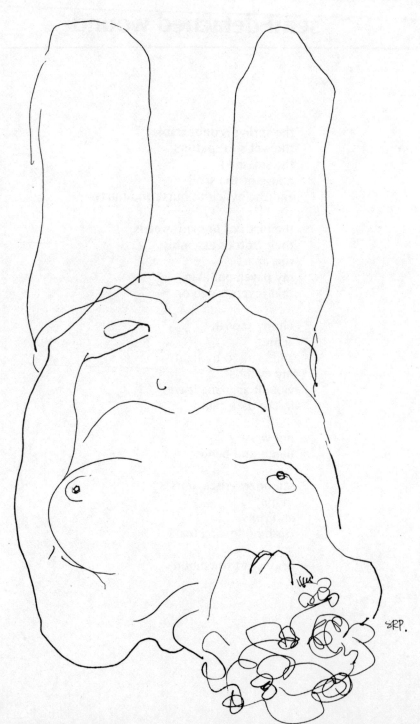

the big man

I want to spin you, big man
make you skip
hop, twirl on nimble toes
I want to whip you like a top
my tongue lashing you
with ropes of silk
till you unfurl
flags, flowers, parasols

I want to be a crazy blackbird
singing all night lewd
riddles to your smiling ear

won't you make my blood
jump? won't you
step along up there
clowning and glittering
beneath the big top, and
see me stretched out here
your fine strong net
with nothing on but jewels?

boom! go the drums of sweat
as neon bodies wink

big man, you hold me in your hands
big man, you warm me with your tender flesh
you are a bee hauling honey out
a fly tickling a slow fish

tulips

the clamped bud
splits, green armour clangs
down, raw scarlet silk
flares like a parachute

the petals' mouth
those red doors
the way in

stamens and pistils burst
up, each sticky velvet brush
gold pollen glistens on
their black fur tips

deep winy heart
as dark as raspberries
for plundering wasps

translucent sun-traps
colour running like a hot
streak of shiny sweet
juice in tossing cups

season of passionate red
opening, red
festival of flames and tongues

falling and flaying
at the same time
in their little
frenzied deaths

lullaby

you're the night watchman, fingers swimming
cloaked along dark streets, you spill
lantern light on flesh, slow
guardian of my city's
deepest cellars, round and round you go
you're familiar with my doorway
every hour this summer night
my cones of lilac burn, and drip
like candles, you call out
all's well, all's well

you're the nightingale
you're the cock at dawn

you're the bruiser, boy, you lust and leap
you scale your mother's lap
like hills in el dorado, leave
home for ever till tomorrow
when she lets you slip, and slaps
you swarm up apple trees, steal fruit
rip legs off flies

you're the pirate baby
you're the mouth at the sweet wine

you're the night fisherman, you push
long finger boats along canals
you slide, exploring, inbetween the river's lips

and you're the man
who pleasures all my locks with oil
who has the key, who knows the way
in, and who hears me call
all's well, all's well

TINA REID

dry rock number

He's lean
He's clean

He's boney
He's stoney

I want to grow his cock
Until it breaks into flower
Wild roses   Dog roses

He's spare
He's bare

I want a garden in his face
Mountains in his eyes
And rivers coursing through his hair

But all he does is come
and go
And he goes
Even faster than he comes

He's a flower
Under glass

He's a scream
In a box

I want to green his intestine
And cultivate his kidneys
See his liver spring into leaf

He's a lark
On crutches

I want to silver birch his skin
Weave willows of his limbs
And climb into his heart of oak

But all he does is come
And go
And he goes
Even faster than he comes

He doesn't know
Who can show

Make him see
Never me

The next one.
Maybe.

spook

She's not the woman she was . . .
She's not the woman he wants.
He wants the woman she was.
He thinks. She was.

At this distance she can pass
For poet, intellectual and page 3-er.
It is thus in her interests
To keep her distance.

But she's not half the woman she was . . .
More like twice.
What genial buttocks
He's let slip through his fingers!

On the other hand
The luscious fruit of compliance
Has dried to a hard nut,
A natural remedy that sticks in the throat.

hanging on for dear life

Oh I've got my hands full alright —
Arms and legs too!
Catching holding stroking
Retrieving feeding poking
Running juggling begging —
I could go on.

And do.
Though sometimes I wonder
If all my tender pink possibilities
Haven't long ago found their feet
And used them,

If all I grasp in my iron glove
Is a bouquet of dry umbilical cords
And black placentas.

dear Sophie

letter to an ill child

One day my eyes will grow
Too tired for crying.
I long for it.

I want them lizardy.
Dry hard and nimble,
Seeing everything.

I want to put
One foot after the other
Through this city,

Through my days,
Through my children's days,
Seeing everything dry.

I want the next juice
Anywhere near to spring
Flowers in my sockets

crossing the Bay of Biscay

There's daily trouble in my world.

Daily, the same victory, the same defeat.
Each day we rock and roll, sedately,
Round the sun, a scheduled sailing:
Whatever the weather, we run on time.

Each day the moon makes a play
To pull us close, to seduce stone.
This poor power nags only at oceans,
Twitches just the skirts of my world.

I grasped the facts in school.
Rolling now through the dark,
Traversing now this perceptive deep heart,
I clutch the facts like mother's skirt.

What could be grander than the galactic weather?
What could be safer than the global routine?
A baby still splashing in its womb
Could not be more spoilt, more cherished!

As ever, I wanted to jump ship.

SPP

letter to a dead woman

Upstairs my friends are making love
With a slap and kiss of swollen labia
And the wallop of well flesh —
The plaster's tinkling in the walls with it.

Elsewhere, alone, put away from me,
You, lips bloating, flesh alive,
Your small house is loud
With the creep and sigh of putrefaction.

I've cried for you once
Hard and quick. Shushed then,
I nursed you like a grievance
Until my lover should come.

I meant to take you into bed
With the pair of us. I would have
Held you while he held me. I wanted to
Give birth to you dead in my bed.

But I laid you down unloved.
I looked away and paid in pleasure
The weekly instalment:
My life insurance, my credentials.

He and I, the tally-man and I,
Are safe on opposite sides.
But my friend and I, oh you and I,
We're trapped

And on opposing sides.

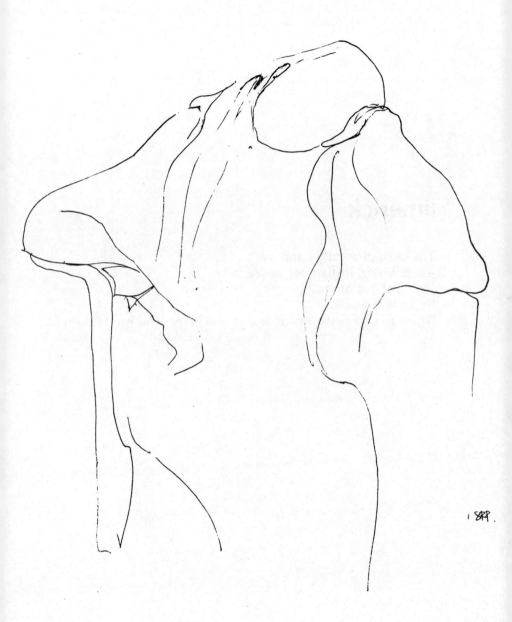

63

limerick

The kids, their father and me
Are bobbing, lost apples, at sea,
Just, just out of reach,
No known beach.
Which to save first? Which to bite first? And who will save me?

a walk through the mountains in northern spain

It is as if the world begins all over again
Three thousand feet up the side of the sky
In plainer fabrics and on different terms.

The top of the cliff
Turns out to be a bottom:
The safe low
That grows the real peaks.

They stalk me
Like pairs of patriarchal thighs
But menace less
Than the space they leave between them.

Weather occurs below:
Winds ambush, clouds sidle
From below.

The sun hangs around like a warder.
The snow can stare it out,
But colours are absent under the eye
Of limestone and sky.

Mountains in midsummer,
Like the undead,
Cast no shadows.

They smell of nothing.
They are silent
Unless the wind smacks their faces
And starts their bellowing.

Their valleys are abrupt:
Upturned hollow peaks,
Monstrous ice-cream cones
Lined with unknowable fathoms of snow.

To walk their greasy walls
I must undress. Abandon children
                              lovers
                              guilt
                              desire
                              dreams of change
                              fear of change.
I can take only myself.

Ice nudges an elbow
And shutters half the sky.
At the other nothing
Occludes the distant low sparkle.

I realise, I remember, that my feet
Are my chief connection with the planet
And that I must place them only and exactly
In the following order:
One after the other,

Calves, thighs, hips
Articulated precisely
On the basis of their information,
While heart and soul are carried,
Cradled, useless potentates.

It's a nightmare it's a meditation it's a life saver.

We sat in the small shade of a rock
On a rock island with the snow at low tide.
My friend scratched out our names
To beat under next winter's drifts.

We left ourselves in the mountains
And came down to our campers'
Separate soft coffins.

I shook still to feel only rock
Beneath the incidental grass beneath my shoulder,
To smell only space through the thin night weather,
To know again, that in all shared experience,
Love, separation, dreams of revolution,
There is only myself for danger or ecstasy.

the journey from Quetta[*]

bed-time story

Those days he would come to bed
In protective clothing
Out of respect
For my feelings. He said
"I'll tell you what happened
After Quetta. I'll hold you
Close and tell you." Instead.

I'll tell you what happened
"After Quetta". I got pregnant.
I fell pregnant every two days.
Sometimes every day I fell,
Pregnant with desire.
I grew heavy, carrying
So many small corpses.

We didn't bother to make love in the city:
Everything you want's in the shops.
And we'd kept nothing
Of the tender summer,
Pickled nothing sharp,
Preserved nothing sweet.
We'd consumed the lot.

I did accomplish some crying.
I turned lardy and
Whitened in brine.
He salted me away,
Against the day
Of another journey, to share
With other companions.

*a border town en route to Afghanistan

queer fish

A warm fish,
curved flipper
in the crook of my body,
settles my stomach.

A goldfish, flash fish,
tentative turner,
unholdable beauty,
leaves me bubbles.

A soft and silverfish
skedaddles round corners
on safari after dark,
making maps of me.

A slippery customer,
sexy swimmer,
guzzles and gurgles
between my legs.

An arched salmon
inspects his tail,
oblivious doughnut,
my lifebelt in river races.

A tricksy tiddler,
perfect minnow,
clever miniature,
escapes my jam jar.

Happy dolphin.
Fast mover.
High leaper.
Smiler. Friend.

he may be a photograph of himself

He is beautiful and still
And unmarked from within,
A mountain in winter,
A loch at dusk.

I sat in his lee
Sharpening flints,
Words to lead
The assault on his rock-face.

I stood on his shore,
Hurling stone
After stone
And did not break his surface.

It will take a disaster,
A mining enterprise,
A dam-burst,
Or a betrayal

To show him,
To know him,
To see the change
I made.

heavy luggage

I once knew a man
Whose penis led him everywhere,
A merry dance.

I knew another
Who had to take his out daily,
Rain or shine.

And still another with another
Whose escapades he endured
Ruefully.

Today, two million pricks
Are riding, meek as lap dogs,
The Motorways One to Six.

A lorry driver, captain of his cab,
Makes forty tons tango to his touch,
And the miles yield, nations surrender
To his wheels.

The Sun beams, the Mirror reflects,
The radio reminds what the posters teach
At the Services, They're all lovable.
Underneath.

He once met a woman
Who did not speak the language.
She forced him to rape her

The M's One to Six
Snake and insist and
Come again and again
On the belly of Britain.

I should like to leave the motorway
And find soft forestry places to love.

Or a citadel of rock and weather,
Or sky that heals fast
From the curlew's long scratch.

I mean always to sing of the best of you,
To see only the whole of you.

But the road the road the road insists.

ALISON FELL

stripping blackcurrants

On a garden rug tinged with amber
your bare skin
grows a red fur.
Half a lilac leaf
sticks to your belly.

Stripping blackcurrants, the berries
split
and stain my fingers
as the stalks
tear from the fruit.

I have a yellow mane which crackles
and brown breasts
freckled as eggs.

Pushing among the leaves, I imagine
their feather fingers
as deft as yours.

Your body haunts the corner
of my eye:
books, papers, your bent head.
I want you in heat,
sticky as blackcurrants.

Deep in the tang of the bush
I remember the taste of your ear.
How you angled your neck
to offer it.

I flaunt my golden back.
It glows from within, a raging aura.
Unbelievable, how you resist me.

You read.
The bush catches fire.

sail away

Sail away, tough mama,
you never were the starlight
mama of my dreams.

How short your legs are:
on the street your little feet
trot: clip clop. How irritating
to slow my pace for you.
I go in bounds.

But you were the one who slipped away
joking, through the check-in,
and soon you'll span the sky.
It's all topsy-turvy,
there are holes just everywhere.

We never suited each other
and we don't fit yet.
I rattle at the stones you
won't look under;
you see a queer stick,
odd daughter,
a questioning thing.

The experiment's over
The wings tear the plane
from the ground.
We must be steel now, for our
separate adventures —
a right pair of steam-hammers,
and the pact lies in that.

So hold steady, tough mama,
sail away,
You never were the starlight mama of my dreams.

friend

In the white morning
we cuddle in our warm
world, toes friendly
in a hoard of blankets,
thighs glossing each other,
bums amiable. Me, I am starved
as a sparrow
after the long cold,
while the snow drives at
tree-trunks,
whirls at my window-sashes,
so fine
it spins
in the cracks and corners
of my house.

Up here
we are in a high galleon
on the crust
of a vanished country.
The sky is iron
behind birds, the road
a track of ash, cracking with
salt, and a scrape and
bang of spades echoes against
the black blocks of streets.

This light
bleaches and blues
skin; our noses of frost
collide.

You are no bully
to dig and spoil, but still
I warn you, some paths
are closed, impassable.

Between my house and yours
lies a city of snowfields;
still I need your steady
heat to set against
the bitterness of winter.

city lights I

I had been weeping and spitting out
the sick talk of snakes
and death;
the night was foul yellow
and the fog whispered of
river bridges.
Each man who winked
had a killing in his eye.
Come on then, come and get me,
I'm weary of putting my fists up.
I could be shameless, loose
my skin and let it drop,
to welcome in the velvet
armies of the night.
For how deep the dark goes in
and all the lights melt into one
and all the lights melt into one

city lights II

Christmas

Space race:
Oxford Street was eyes of glass,
astronauts, a Sugar-Plum fairy,
a window blinking with televisions.

Red laser beams pierce the street:
sight fails in splinters
before the sparkling jig of atoms,
the creation of Coherent Light*
targetting past the horizon.
Eyes and hearts have limits
that have been reached.

The televisions flicker and fix:
the Earth is a blue balloon,
men dance the muffled
dance of toys on the dry rock
and suck at the dust of the moon
and suck at the dust of the moon

*Coherent Light is the scientific name given to the light which composes laser beams

desire

The wind is strong enough to move wasps.
This blowing branch is mine,
silvery thing, all mine,
my teethmarks swarm over it:
what sweet sap and small beetles racing.

Mother warns me I will get worms
from this zest
for chewing and digesting
fur buds and the satin
leaves of beech, from all this
testing and possessing.
'Stop that' she says,
'Stop this minute. See the
wee eggs you'll swallow!'

My needle-bright eye is rash
and scans greedily,
sees pine-cones lose pollen
in yellow gusts;
the loch's rim has a
curd of it, the face of
the middle deeps is
skimmed with dust and wrinkles.

The birch trunk wears a
sleeve of paper, clear-layered,
like sunburned skin — a wrap.
It streams from my thumbnail
till the wind snatches it.

period madness

Oh, when the taps jut
and piano stools leap to bite
and your thighs — fat waterbags —
bruise to rainbows, and,
balance gone,
you twirl in a cauldron
reeking of nastiness,
and the spine shrieks
and neglect aches
and time is a swamp to crawl through
till the tide bursts,
and you steam up the street
with elbows angled,
taking swathes —
See me, I am a plougher
of men on the packed pavements,
greasy, snarling,
ready to flail.

suspicion

This terrible alertness
sours the milk in me,
binds lips, tears
a barb across the heart.
What is to be trusted
if mothering breeds
hatred at the core?
This pap and pretence
is bitter food.

What is to be hoped for
when the lovely twist
of hawthorns
warns
only of trickery,
and bark peels
to a pith of spite?

My grim eye strips
the gifts women bring
and in the bread and smiles
sees hidden worms lie.

yorkshire dales, easter

(for Marsha)

We walked in moonland
while the grouse raged at us
black peat sprung our heels
white silt of limestone seeped

and everywhere a rumble of change:
landslips, frogs' spawn,
ooze of sap.

Walking side by side was easy,
with no shocks
the land could not absorb.

Diverting you,
I poked at lichens,
at tree-clefts
that rot or ants had chewed.

But then the shyest hand in the world
reached over.
I sought it, I feared it —
careful kiss of friendship,
woman to woman. This time,
you were close in.

I thrust will against the flinch,
breathed air,
leaned into this extraordinary
faltering bond.
(Grumble of change, whispers
in the bracken
where no wind shook it.)

I was dizzy, trying to laugh or swallow,
on these elephant rocks,
on that scarp where the sky
wheeled over.

surface tension

1. Since she was warned of the danger
   her belly holds desire like a
   bomb in the back seat of a car.
   Her skin too thin for collisions
   is a diaphragm dividing chemicals.

2. Ten days of the month she is
   lustier than any hero, yeasty,
   all cunt. Her glycerine hips
   hint and swagger. She's a huntress;
   a knife grins in her teeth.
   but her hands are tied.

3. On the surface they stalk tall,
   the tension webbing them.
   She turns tail, diving for
   avenues of grass, to nose
   among slugs for the wet secrets
   of dawn and mushrooms.
   Or seeking air, she leaps too high
   and skims in the chinks
   of the gates of day
   in her new blue iridescent madness.

lanarkshire 1949

The comb drags
the washcloth is roughly wielded
the pudding is a mess of raisins —
yet there is no cause for complaint.
The fierce girl so silenced
turns poltergeist:
in her magic mechanics
wishes are piledrivers.
So if the pit-bing* slips
or the eggs tumble and break,
who else is responsible
but the four-year-old
with the torn hem,
who trails in gangs
to yell at Papes,
and raids allotments
for a fistful of strawberries.
In this stew of darkness,
thoughts can spit.
The mother may crumple at the cabbage pot
and the bed in the alcove
burn to hell.

*Scottish for slag-heap

the weight

Whole days gone while
the world goes on and I
go under;
carpets have interstices,
floors are quicksands,
bottomless

down, down, the lead baby
goes dangling,
to plumb caverns where
the woman-mountain waits.
Still stone she draws
me down

— let me go, let me grow older

as rocks we rub, hopeless,
scarring each other.
It is a mothering cold as death
and incoherent,
here, without air or sun or sap.
She will wear me round her neck
for years yet,
ugly ornament which clanks
and chafes

— let me go, let me lighten,
let my breasts drift up
like dry leaves.

in confidence

(for the Writers' Group)

— An orgasm is like an anchovy,
she says,
little, long, and very salty.

— No, it's a caterpillar,
undulating, fat and sweet.

— A sunburst, says the third,
an exploding watermelon:
I had one at Christmas.

— Your body betrays, she says,
one way or another.
Rash and wriggling, it comes
and comes, while your mind
says lie low, or go.

— Or else it snarls and shrinks
to the corner of its cage
while your mind, consenting,
whips it on and out,
out in the open
and *so* free.

— As for me,
says the last,
if I have them brazen
with birthday candles,
with water faucets
or the handles of Toby Jugs,
I don't care who knows it.
But how few I have —
keep *that* in the dark.

deer forest

the blue pines shiver
under fighter planes
the cornfields are cut to white
the rosehips a red arch above me

be quiet
I am listening
for the scratch of antlers

how many trees crushed
to make those letters
you choke me with?
paper flags stabbing at me
paper aeroplanes

be quiet
I am waiting
in the still place under the bridge
I am waiting
for the sky to rush

I am the star you desire in hatred
to name
to stamp
to claim
I am the flint underfoot to savage
your mad goat's heels

heart of april

Upside down
in a magnolia tree
I dangle
in a sea of heaped sky
a soup
brimming with white flowers.

The sky is full of fevers,
greenbronze,
colour of dragons,
and in the city streets
the sour thunder dust
as the air
bears low.

Dissatisfaction sounds
like an axe
cracking sticks.
I am narrowed down to bones
shin bones across his legs
bones sticking in his teeth.

I will not be a midden-hen,
thin and grubbing.
I am winged and webbed
I am bigger than this.
Bright, formless, fluctuating.

and again

The man with the big mouth
and the ribbon-elastic legs
has bowled me over

His tongue running in my mouth
is sweet as a bean

The bare branch of his forearm
sets me sweating.
My pores open: no shelter

He's a dark man,
melancholic and bitter;
with a hornet's sting
he bites to the bone

Dreadful in suspicion,
he becomes a leech
— he will have me,
he sings it to the telephone wires

Since last year I've grown
cautious
and knowledgeable:
ruefully I refuse him

The child stamps and wails out,
mourning the trust of his fragrance —
the true skin,
indisputable
as jasmine in the dark

sunday in february

An apple bitten once
and spat in the gutter
glows bright
it is past, it is wasted

The corpse must go fully dressed
into the fire
with its Sunday shoes shining
it is past, it is wasted

Work, meetings, motherhood,
the discipline of hours and service
stretch thin in the running rain
oh, it could all snap
like a black bootlace

I could die on Sundays
and lie clotted and cold

while the rain washes
the ashes of my father
down the slate sides of the mountains

the well

Down there my reflection hangs
small rose-head
dead-looking

The rope chokes
The world is a dry bed

I am empty
Go deeper

What will come on hooks and footholds
up from the well?

The bucket hurtles
smashing the surface
the agitation goes on and on
the ripples intersect and are circular

Force turns the axle

The bucket comes up
swings
splashes
sparkles

There is a river of light in each drop
which runs
clings
whistles down
rings in the deep place

The lips of a well
are the sharpest of edges
EXHILARATION

ANN OOSTHUIZEN

leaving town

Veronica and I paused before entering the main door of the university. The bright outdoors was sucked into the cold building where it was turned gloomy by brown linoleum and dark walls. We glanced back and saw Adrian behind us. He stood at the bottom of the steps in the sunlight, his blue shirt bright against the granite wall.

We could see the town spread out behind him. A gravel path led straight down to the arched university gate and its surrounding buildings, once soldiers' quarters and goal, now white-washed monument. From there the path became a road which ran smack into the cathedral, with shops and insurance offices clustered under its spire. Making a wide loop around the cathedral, the road continued down to the squat, grey station, then veered left to suburbia, schools and playing fields. To the right and behind the station were narrow streets and dirt tracks, left-overs from the past, or barnacle development on the white town. Overcrowded, rusty tin shacks, dry yards, swollen-bellied children and hairless, bony dogs were common sights. behind the railway station. The road seemed to sense this and beckon the traveller away towards clipped lawns and flowering rose-bushes, healthy youngsters in cricket togs and dinner party conversation on the cost of living or *The Four Quartets*.

Once, the students had gone down the path and under the arch in an angry swarm, marching simply against the loss of their right to make such a protest. They were stopped before they reached the cathedral; they had had no intention of going beyond it. Adrian had not gone with them even so far, had wanted to join them, but feared too great a commitment to ideals and causes might destroy his cosy domestic clutter. He was coming up the steps.

"Shall we wait for him?"

"No." How much longing in that one word. But to wait, like a beggar at the gate, to see him turn away, see him pretend no knowledge. Carnal knowledge; no bond.

Of course I had heard the arguments. Marriage is a sacred institution which demands the blood sacrifice of all those who question its perfection.

Who did I think I was anyway daring to come between husband and wife? I cowered in doorways, watching the married couples parade past, with prim mouths set against me, a representaive of chaos who did not know her place.

Indeed, my place was what it was all about. In the antique settler newspapers printed a century ago and framed under glass in the town museum, a widow is desribed as a relic. No longer living and breathing among the dancing couples in society, joined discreetly to the grave, she is entertained at less important functions, where the male power is as absent as the smell of polished shoe leather or Boxer tobacco, although the talk is still a happy assumption of married felicity. I had refused this miserly friendship, had demanded that our family, what was left of it, should not be shut away from life.

As a result our house was visited by frightened, confused students and black intellectuals. Like me they had nowhere else to go. The big white house stood in the white suburbs. Open to late-night callers, it was watched suspiciously by neighbours and officially by the secret police. Nevertheless we were comfortable there. The rooms were warmed by many visitors, who brought their friends, who stayed overnight on journeys across the country, who debated earnestly the future of the different races, who laughed and wept together. Yet I had decided to leave this fortress because it represented the privileges I gained by being white. Although I was stripping myself of all the goods that had accumulated in my name, I had hoped to go away armed with Adrian's regard. I had not realised that I should have to leave his love behind also.

Veronica always wore black. Her long blonde hair hung heavy and straight, past a pale, strained face. Her hands clutched cigarettes and matches. She knew and felt my confusion and her sympathy was unspoken. There was enough said by others anyway.

We walked together. The lecture we were about to attend was a popular one so the corridor was filled with students and members of staff from the Departments of English, Politics and Anthropology. The speaker, David Ross, was a black man, a scholar and writer, who would present his view of Black Consciousness, Black Power and all those black people who were wild enough to say the white man was shit. His audience would be members of our whites-only university, who upheld concepts like academic freedom in a society where only whites had such freedom and then only if they chose their subjects carefully.

David was a short, stocky man, well-built and dressed in his Magdalen College blazer and tie. His strong handsome face was suave and confident. He had been received in town like a hero: staying with the Professor of English, he was honoured as a visiting black writer. Initiate in South African literature, he had, with a party from the English Department, climbed a bare Karoo mountain to pay his respects to Olive Shreiner's grave. Thus accepted he came to speak to us.

The sun slanted into the room through the big windows overlooking the town. There were so many people it was difficult to find a seat. Veronica and

I sat gloomily at the back. As the lecturer ascended the rostrum, the busy audience became quiet. Faces turned expectantly towards him. How did he see the great black beast rearing itself to consciousness, accusing us at last of the murder perpetrated on its ancestors and all their descendants to this very day? He would give us the answer. Black himself and therefore qualified to speak, he would tell us. Here, in the centre of our institution, the main lecture hall of the Arts and Administration block, he would bring us the key to what our attitude should be to those concepts which by their very names excluded us from the start — Negritude, Black Consciousness — which made a glory out of what had been despised for generations and rejected us and our version of what it meant to be committed intellectuals.

Well, let's not take this phenomenon seriously. Let us play over it lightly with some Oxford wit, sneer at Sartre's mawkish romanticism, coolly dismiss Senghor et al. Reading sarcastically from the poetry and prose of emergent Africa, he rejected it as a masquerade for maniacs. He, of course, knew what civilisation and the great tradition was about. A realist, he wrote for cash, not to explore, to analyse or to convert. His objectivity would be rewarded by a chair at Harvard in Afro-American Studies. Thus the black experience becomes a focus for academic credits.

The fat tick sucks the blood of the thin cattle.

Members of the audience jumped up to express their appreciation of the speaker's views. They were so happy to hear such a comprehensive talk. What, they asked, were his views on Fanon? And of course, Mtshali was not a true poet, his language, they agreed, was thin, without resonance; he was really only a township politico, a literary opportunist. Everyone was smiling now. How nice to have found a black man just like us. How exciting to meet a successful writer whose play had been broadcast on the BBC World Service!

I had sat next to David at a dinner-party the previous evening. I thought back to what he had said then. He had laughed at Catherine, whom we both knew. What a bore she was! How ridiculous and stupid to involve her friends when she had wilfully got herself into trouble with the police. When she came seeking help she only endangered others.

Catherine, arrested without trial, alone in a cell for over a hundred days, haunted by visions of private sins, crazed in her isolation by weakness and guilt, crawled on the floor for fear of the gas she suspected was being pumped through the ceiling. Catherine, her bones poking out of her thin flesh, convalescent from an illness which would never leave her after those dreadful days, walked weakly in exile through the English lanes, her fire reduced now to a pitiful chirp at all creation, her shaking hands and sleepless nights the price she still paid for wanting change. Her interrogators laughed and called her an ostrich because her longing for freedom was so great that she swallowed broken glass and buttons off her clothes in a effort to break open the doors of their hearts so that they would let her go. On her release, when she was no longer useful to them, they advised her to see a doctor.

And David, dark and smooth, with the body of a sportsman, handsome and sure of his position: of course Catherine was unbalanced. A typical white lady trying to salve her consience. What a joke she was.

Veronica sat seething with fury. "The usual detente situation where you only dialogue with those who will sell out anyway," she muttered. As if to prove her point, David was now talking comfortably on first name terms with the academic leaders of what had once, in *The Spectator*, been described quite seriously as the worst university in the world. He and Brian, our Professor of Politics, whose liberal activism had survived only as a souvenir, shared a light for their cigarettes.

The speaker had satisfied his audience and was being taken to tea. Veronica and I wanted to break through his confident veneer to some discussion of what was involved in his presence at the university. I moved quickly up to him, walking alongside him to draw his attention.

"Excuse me, David . . . "

"Oh. Hello . . . "

"May I introduce Veronica?" He stopped momentarily, charmed to meet her. Veronica hid her anger under a tight smile.

"Would you say those things at Fort Hare? The black students there would certainly give your talk a very different reception to what it received today."

He replied at once: "I don't give speeches. I do not have the time. I am a writer."

"Don't you realise how valuable Black Consciousness is in this country? It helps the people to assert their will."

Again the quick, defensive reply: "Sheer nonsense. Look where I am. There is no need for ill-formulated ideas."

He regretted his friendliness and tried to edge away. Walking fast along the corridor, we had already reached the stairs and were descending towards the entrance and the Senior Common Room.

Veronica pressed him: "Can't you see what you are doing, saying such things now and in this place? Look how pleased all these whites are to have you bolster their comfortable liberalism. You feed their need to be relevant. You affirm their position."

Tea-time.

We had come to rest outside the Senior Common Room. The debate could have continued, but David was clearly put out and Adrian, without acknowledging my presence, came to rescue him. The swing doors shut in our faces as they disappeared inside to join at tea our philosopher manque, our local playwright and our new American lecturer in Politics, ex-CIA.

We stood there adrift, unable to move from where we had been interrupted; Veronica was a student, we were joined by two tutorial assistants, all of them were forbidden access to the tea-urn, although at this time of day the Common Room was practically deserted. Those inside knew they could win every round by using the power given to them by the institution which was backed by an approving community of which they were the leaders.

In the past I would have gate-crashed the tea-party and brought my friends with me on the strength of my position as a lecturer in the university, but I had lost confidence. The beloved looks at you and you are whole and proud, he looks away, and almost from that moment you cease to exist for yourself and for those friends you had in common. Adrian had chaired the meeting, now his mouth would be formulating the words best suited to invest the occasion with metaphysical resonance. His eyes blinking, he would finger his beard or light a cigarette, pausing thus to emphasise the earnestness of his commitment. Those who were with him would nod attentively as I had so often done. He was launched, his voyage charted, and had left me like a piece of garbage, discarded from a passing ship, spilled up on the open beach. I was too beaten to fight this image, accepting the valuation.

"Let's buy some People's brandy," said Veronica. But it was hard to reach the people, who lived beyond the railway station in the neglected wasteland outside the town. We didn't belong there and would not know our way. Besides, our white faces would have made us an easy target for the secret police. "And what are you doing here lady?" they would say when they stopped us, "Have you a permit to enter the location?".

So we sat on my big brass bed and smoked, giggling tearfully as we shared the joint. Downstairs the house was being stripped of furniture. As I prepared to leave town, the rooms were emptied, the polished floors showed bare and open, the house became hushed, its life ending. I moved carpets and chairs in an effort to fill the space, but soon the emptiness would win.

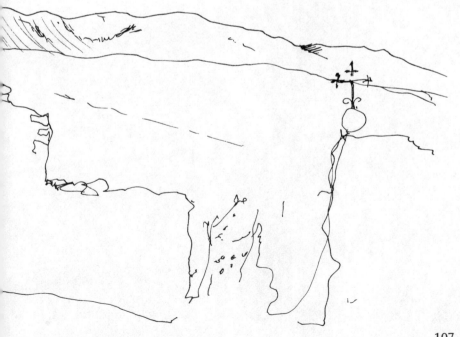

five women

This story is dedicated to five women who died between summer 1976 and summer 1977. Cheryl, age 23, Isobel, age 80, Lee, age 24, Pauline, age 36, Catherine, age 44.

When I looked out of the window in response to Cheryl's ring, her pale face turned up to me in the darkness. It was already after 11, could she have a bath, she asked.

She sat talking in my room. Her long hair was spread over her shoulders to dry. She picked at her life like someone pulling out thorns.

She wrote: "I cannot accept myself for what I am. I am tired of being me."

Outside the crematorium the snow falls briefly on cypress and landscaped grass, the dingy waiting room colder than charity.

When Isobel died they laid her out on the narrow bed and covered her face with a sheet. In the room the silence was like snow. They had brushed her hair back from her face, leaving it free of all vanity. We left two red roses on the white sheets, hoping thus to reach through her resolute absence.

Her body was still bandaged to cover the cancer. I had seen it first and smelled it a month before when she had taken the overdose. She did not know that I gagged so much at the smell of her body that I could not put on the dressing. It was the day they took her to hospital.

The doctor was displeased to be called away from surgery. We sat in the next room and could hear her beg: "Kill me, kill me . . ." She wanted the sanction of his help.

"No!" he shouted at her.

It was the fifth time in three weeks that Lee had turned up at the hospital to have her stomach pumped. The nurses laughed and made fun of her, saying she was hooked on the pump. The doctor sent her carelessly home. That night she drowned in the fluid in her lungs.

Pauline pinned her name to her dress before she jumped, so that there would be no trouble identifying her body. She had a tidy, incisive mind. At home she looked after two small children and read *Oedipus Rex* for the English degree she was doing by correspondence. She remained silent while her husband talked.

I imagine these women standing stiffly, like a Byzantine frieze. I rush to catch buses, catch cold, read theory of women's oppression. Their eyes look past me. Their deaths sever my contact with them.

I am in Marks and Spencer, looking for a skirt and blouse for Isobel. I look for her size. Almost I find myself buying a particularly suitable jacket. I stop myself from buying clothes for a dead woman.

What a coincidence, I say, that in this last year four women I have known, not acquaintances merely, but women that I have known, have chosen to die. And even as I say this the angle of the frieze enlarges, I hear of another death.

Catherine died thirteen years ago in a prison cell in South Africa. She was held in solitary confinement so that the police could extract a statement from her. The tape recordings they had taken of conversations in her flat revealed intimately the guilt she felt for the death of her twin sister. Her interrogators reviled her for being a jewess. After three months she crawled on the floor of her cell for fear of the gas crystals she imagined descending from the ceiling and drank the lavatory water because she suspected that she was being poisoned.

She was never called to witness against her friends. When she was released the police recommended that she see a psychiatrist.

I saw her last nine years ago, her hand shaking as she lit yet another cigarette, her arms and legs thin as a Belsen survivor. As we walked in a soft, green English wood, she made small chirping sounds at a little wren in the thicket, a mouse scrambling across dead leaves.

She waited twelve years for her fiancé to be released from prison. He came out old and tired, needing comfort. She had nothing more to give.

Isobel, Cheryl, Pauline, Lee, Catherine, your deaths were so womanly; Sandra wrote: "Whoever finds me, forgive me for my selfishness."

Pauline knew the loneliness of motherhood. Literature, that gallery of ancient monuments is hardly appropriate to the kitchen shelf. Men shape in their imagination the world around them, and sing out of tune. Jocasta, a minor part, mother and wife to Oedipus, realises before he does that they have sinned. A man should not sleep with his mother. She hangs herself, so the story goes. At the climax of the play, Oedipus blinds himself, but is sanctified later because of his great suffering. His daughter dedicates her life to looking after her blind father-saint.

Imagine Pauline's hand, thin and tanned; she had dark hair, her body was delicately boned. Imagine her hand writing her name and address and pinning it carefully to her jacket. She had a choice of names, her father's or her husband's. I wonder whether she thought of this, or whether her name was now nothing more than a posting-box for the body she no longer wanted. That sickening jump. Now you are alive and standing high, looking down. Go. As you crash through the dimensions of time and space is there still anguish? Others use pain killers to die, thus drowsily entering the gates of death, but maybe even then the dreams are pain.

Cheryl was haunted all her life by a recurring dream. She first dreamed it when she was a five-year-old in hospital with jaundice. She screamed so much the doctors sent her home, preferring rather to quarantine the entire block in which she lived than cope with her fear.

In the dream she was alone in a room, but became aware that in the far corner crouched a monstrous being who drew her to him by some power he had over her. She knew friends were close by, yet she was certain that they would be unable to help her.

Beyond this creature was darkness. She screamed herself awake so that she could escape from him.

In the last year of her life this dream recurred frequently. She was afraid to go to sleep. The night she left me she found someone else in the street she could talk with until it was light.

I walk past the ruins of the slum she once lived in. Determined that she would have a place which belonged only to her, where no man could throw her out if he grew angry with her or tired of her, she had squatted a flat of her own in a building which would soon come down, where the smell of piss on the landings, the broken glass and dirty, peeling paint discouraged visitors.

Now the outside walls are down; lacerated by the wreckers the soft interior walls show bits of wallpaper or a fireplace hanging in mid-air. I wonder if this was the room she had decorated to die in.

Lee lived in other people's rooms. I took her flowers before she had the abortion. They were tight, pale daffodils in a narrow bunch. She jerked a smile across her face to hide her terror.

She was returned to Belfast after dying in London. Friends accompanied her. The funeral service was in church (her family was Protestant) where all wept for her brilliant future.

A voluntary exile from her own country, her involvement in left-wing politics and with the men who led them, gave her no more comfort than that dead child.

Cheryl was a foster child. She had, by chance, made love to her own brother. He took her to his home where she met her biological mother. She tried, through fairy stories, to create a world which was not governed by caprice, but which had a logic that corresponded to her ideals.

"There stood poor Gerda without shoes or gloves in the middle of the bitter cold of Finland. She ran as fast as she could. A regiment of gigantic

111

snowflakes came against her, but they melted when they touched her, and she went on with fresh courage."

At Cheryl's funeral her family huddles together, their sobs rising in a collective crescendo as the coffin disappears theatrically behind a screen of mock marble to the strains of taped *Jesu Joy of Man's Desiring*. No, no, Cheryl, wails auntie Jean in a groan flawed with self-regard.

I too am tired of being me. I want to be younger, beautiful, bionic, without the weight of these deaths on me. I am chained to an ageing body that bleeds heavily each month. Today I bleed again. Every half hour I change the tampon; it is soggy with blood. If I am lazy, busy, forgetful, the blood seeps through my pants, through my dress, leaving dark stains. The tops of my thighs show water-marks of blood. When I walk I leave drops of crimson on the floor that must be cleaned up with bits of toilet paper or cotton wool. My muscles ache as the blood drains out of my body.

Isobel believed that womanhood is tenderness, generosity, nobility. Sacrifice was necessary, she said, it would not do to complain about it. Each month we bleed for the children waiting to be born.

Yet we are ashamed of this bleeding because the men we love do not bleed like us and find the fluids that come from our bodies disgusting. The Snow Queen does not bleed.

I walk again in the dingy street where Cheryl had taken refuge. The building has gone. It is after the wreckers, but before the developers, the office blocks are still on paper. Cheryl makes way for the autumn sunlight. We are ashamed of our pain, our misery only adds to the gloom. Don't make a fuss, hide, die.

Isobel woke early in the morning to wash in secret the bandages she used to bind her cancerous wound.

Isobel fed the birds. The neighbour's dog was not turned away. When her illness made all chores a burden, she worried anxiously that there would not be enough food in the house, she stocked the refrigerator with ten pounds of butter, five dozen eggs, twenty packets of suet. When visitors were expected she planned obsessively what what they eat, seeing them as appetites that must be fed, a monstrous image of an insatiable world demanding food from her, demanding shelter.

I listen to the latest unemployment figures on the late night news. Sleep princess, the wicked fairy counsels, sleep now for we have no need of you this next hundred years.

Catherine's statement to the United Nations is filed away under 'Treatment of Political Prisoners in South Africa'.

So five women died, five women who did not know each other, but who whom I knew. Their blood spills out unheeded on the dark streets, runs down the walls of banks, spreads across the billboards, creeps up the lift shafts in the tall buildings. I meet a woman who gets up at 4 a.m. to clean the offices of the National Coal Board. She earns so little that the Welfare Department pays her rent. The reality is nothing like they told us. So Cheryl puts on her black dress in her painted room, she sleeps through the noise of the city and dreams further into that nightmare dream.

I take Isobel's ashes back to Africa to the place where she spent her childhood. They are in my baggage in a small silver cigarette box, tied up with a piece of string. At various places on my journey, I stop for a few days. I unpack the silver case and look at it.

I am an authority on funerals.

Father O'Riley teeters on tiny feet, the river far below us reflects the mountains ten miles away. We are no pagans, he says, praying to his almighty before scattering Isobel's ashes over the precipice. The banks of the river are covered knee-high in grass. She had wanted to end her days in the house we can see standing peacefully in the bend of the river, but her husband had not wished to return.

I weep uncontrollably.

You five women, it is no wonder I keep on expanding your number as I hear of yet another death.Today I read in a newspaper that a young mother has thrown herself out of the window of her high-rise flat. The frieze seems never-ending; the women stand gracefully, silently, even inconspicuously, their hands hold loaves of bread, bunches of flowers, cradles or bundles of washing. They stand over sick beds, over stoves, over clean laundry, over blood-stained sheets.

No, I say to myself. I am a dumpy figure weighed down by two heavy shopping bags. I angle my body homewards against gale-force winds. No, that is not right. I will give meaning to these deaths, but the image I have is too timid, too static, too graceful. Underneath all this litany of names lies my own guilt; I feel guilty that I am still alive, that I am not in that prison cell, on that roof, that I did not put on my black dress in a ritual of death. I have elevated them to sainthood so that I can prostrate myself before them, light candles of words to their memory, bury their raw pain in sentimental pictures.

I feel insensitive that there is still fight left in me, that I find pleasure in the company of other women, that the wild flowers growing in each season bring me joy. The blu hyacinth in the pot on my table unfolds a new bloom each day. When they are all open there is one miraculous flower. I do not feel isolated, will not be silent, but I will light no more candles. Monuments are for the dead we bury. I say the names over again: Cheryl, Lee, Pauline, Isobel, Catherine, my sisters, it is not amazing that you chose to die, it is amazing that other women are still alive, that we survive.

sandra

When I come into the refuge, Penny and Ricky are sitting in the high chairs in the kitchen with plates of cold, grey mush in front of them. They both have on smelly nappies. Their eyes are large, brimming with tears because Sandra, their mother, is out shopping. There are other women in the kitchen. I make myself a cup of tea and sit down near Ricky. June is there, a large, strong woman, Turkish speaking, from Cyprus. She stands above me and makes a dramatic gesture with her arm towards the two children.

"Do you know what these two did last night?" she asks.

"What?"

"They ate their mother's birth pills!"

"Good God! What happened?"

"Sandra was out. We took them to hospital. The doctor says it is OK, but that they will be sick. Penny was sick this morning."

"How many did they take?"

"Sandra didn't know how many she had left. She forgot to take some and then her period started. She didn't know if it was one or two or even twenty!"

I think about the article I have just read in the *New Scientist* which describes how male sex offenders are given female hormones and grow pendulous breasts. Paula says: "Joy took some of my pills once; the doctor said it is all right if a girl takes them, but if a boy takes them he will become sterile."

"Well," June replies, "this doctor says it is all right."

"Did you tell him what kind?" asks Paula.

"We went there and took the packet. Sandra wasn't here. She was out."

Sandra walks into the kitchen. She looks at me.

"Did you hear what these two did last night?"

"I heard," I reply. The children say nothing. I have started feeding Ricky. He is under a year old, with a solemn, round face. When he finishes his cereal, he starts to cry. He smells terrible. Sandra puts away her shopping and sits next to him. She says: "I overslept. The health visitor has got them places in a nursery, but I feel a bit silly taking them so late. I haven't had much sleep lately. Last night it was them taking the pills, and I've got this awful toothache."

"The first day is always the worst. You might as well get it over with, so you can start a routine."

Sandra speaks to Penny: "I'll take Ricky up and clean him and then come down for you. Is that alright?"

Penny nods, but looks tearful. She is almost three with large brown eyes, her hair, a pale ash blonde, is cut short round her face. I feed her. She opens her mouth for each spoonful until the plate is empty. She looks at me and asks: "My mummy is coming back?"

"Yes, as soon as she is finished dressing Ricky," I assure her. She nods, but when she has finished her cereal she starts to cry.

"All right," I respond, "I'll lift you out of your chair, but don't go upstairs yet. Just wait for your mummy to fetch you."

She stands quite still against the table, crying silently. She is wearing a pink nightdress and her feet are bare. She looks like a diminutive adult. I say: "Hang on, I'll just finish my tea and then I'll help you get dressed."

"My mummy won't go without me?"

Mary puts her baby, Karen, into the high chair that Ricky has just left. Karen is a silent baby who hardly ever cries. She is around nine months old, with a small, wizened face and big ears. She is too small for the chair and slips over to one side of it. Mary warms up a bottle of milk.

I put down my mug of tea, which is growing cold, and say: "Come on, Penny, let's go." She takes my hand and we climb the two flights of stairs to the room Sandra, Penny and Ricky share with Mary, Karen and Mary's son Paul, who is seven.

Sandra is still busy with Ricky, but gives us a flannel, towel, pants and vest so we can go down one flight again to the bathroom. I had meant to bathe Penny, but the bath is full of clothes soaking. The bathroom has a stale, mouldy smell. I flush the toilet which has paper and faeces floating in it and start running the water in the basin. I take off Penny's nappy, which means undoing the knots in its plastic covering. The paper towel is sopping wet and dirty. When I roll it up, she announces urgently: "I must sit on the toilet." I help her on and she seems to piss and crap with some relief, as if she has been holding it in.

I wash her face and ears and then take off her nightdress to wash her all over. She does not shiver, although the bathroom is unheated. Nor does she complain about the cold or the discomfort of being washed as I have heard so many children do. When I bend down to wash her legs, I notice four or five livid, round scars on her calves and thighs as well as two purplish weals.

"What happened to you?" I ask.

"Daddy burned me with a cigarette," she replies. Her voice does not change, there is neither anger nor sorrow in it.

"Ricky has one as well," she continues, "Mummy did it. Mummy is waiting isn't she?"

I wrap her in a soft towel and rub her dry. We put on the vest and panties. She runs up ahead of me while I pick up the pink nightdress and the soiled nappy.

In the bedroom, Sandra has just finished dressing Ricky. She is looking for Penny's shoes. Perhaps they were left in June's room, because June bathed her the night before. When Penny is dressed, she flies up to the top floor to get the shoes.

"I'm a bit bothered about the burns on her legs," I remark tentatively.

"Yes, my husband did that. He did it to Ricky as well."

The two children turn to her with gentle, engulfing love. She responds as well as she can, now putting on their coats — a present from a friend's mother — to take them to the nursery. Later, as I see them pass the window, I tap on it and wave to them. Sandra calls to Penny to wave back. Sandra is nineteen years old.

marie looks after herself

When the City Police bring Marie to the refuge, she is wrapped in a blanket which they have lent her because she had run into the Station without a dress or skirt. She is a big woman, youngish, but overweight with straggly, dark hair. She has a baby son, David, who has huge brown eyes with immensely long lashes. He does not yet walk. She carries him with her everywhere she goes and he cries if she puts him down. She tells us that another, older child has been taken into care. She wants to be re-housed in Westminster. When I explain that Westminster Council will only re-house families who have lived in the borough, she says: "But when I'm re-housed I *will* be living there."

At the New Year's Eve party in the refuge, David is upstairs asleep. She confides to me: "I've been on valium for two years. I am a marked sheep."

The women in the house are friendly towards Marie, but wary. Afraid that her strangeness will turn into violence.

She is looking for a light for her cigarette. I tell her there is a candle standing on the telephone box, which is fixed to the wall, but she doesn't understand and Barbara gives her a light. She says to me: "I thought you said there was a telephone on my head."

"No," I say hastily, afraid she is working herself up, "No, I didn't say that."

"I like all the workers and all the women and children here," she goes on, "But there is one thing I don't like, I don't like it when people phone me up. When they do that I must leave. I must go to another refuge."

The week before, the health visitor, a tall, gentle woman, had offered David a place in a nursery. Marie went wild. She stood against the wall near the door with David in her arms shouting that the health visitor had no jurisdiction over her, that she had her own health visitor, that nurseries were the next best thing to taking children into care, that it was just icing on the cake, that she was better than any nursery and didn't need other people to entertain her child. She flounced out still shouting, slammed the door shut leaving the room in ruins behind her.

Tonight she is relaxing, she smiles at me: "The doctor gave me sleeping pills. When my husband bothers me, I put them in his food. That's what the doctor gave them to me for. To look after myself."

The party is becoming louder, drunker. We are playing a complicated game with numbers where there are forfeits and this means a woman has to drink down her drink in one go. Sandra is the one who regularly pays the forfeit. Everyone is laughing and talking. Marie says loudly above the noise: "Once I got drunk and passed out. I pulled off a man's beard."

"Was it false?"

"No, no it was real. That's why he was so angry."

People are doing turns. Barbara and Sandra are in the chorus line. Sandra sings in nasal seduction: "Goodbye Sam, Hello Samantha . . ." She moves her hips to the tune. Marie announces that she will do an Irish jig. She dances with small neat steps, her body upright, her head tilted back, her arms up. Perfectly in control of her own body.

She looks at me.

"Do you know the singer, John McCormick?"

"No."

"He was very popular. Do you know him?"

"No."

"Neither do I."   She laughs.

"He was very popular," she explains, "and good and then he went right *down*," her body folds at the waist, her knees bend in a downward movement, her hands sweep the floor, "Right down." She laughs.

"I'm glad," she says.

Celia, who has access to the cast-off clothes of wealthy women in Hampstead and Finchley, brings them to the refuge. Tonight she has a plastic bag filled with dresses and shoes from expensive shops. "Look," she says to Marie, "These shoes might fit. Try on this dress." Marie puts a pair of pumps onto small, neat feet.

Later Marie goes out more, reappears one day with her hair softly waved, wearing a new outfit, transformed into a beauty. She stays away for longer and longer periods. The last time I see her, she comes in to find out why the Council is so slow in offering her a flat. I advise her to go down to the Housing Bureau to sort it out herself.

"I want to move in before I go on my summer holiday," she says.

home to hackney

It is always difficult for me to understand the allure that Hackney has for the people who live there. Mare Street, for example, it seems to me, is a large, untidy main street with dirty shop fronts and no grace. Great big lorries rumble down it and the buses, like number 30 and 253, are infrequent and take hours along roundabout routes to find their way to other, more accessible parts of London. Yet when Mary and Sally and I find ourselves cruising around Hackney one morning with an hour to spare, Mary is very excited. This was her home ground and she is back on it as from exile, safe because she is in a car, able to be once more in the streets and corners of her childhood.

"That's something else Leroy's done to me," she says. "Taken Hackney from me."

"You don't dare to walk these streets now?"

"No, if he sees me, he'll kill me. He'll never forgive me for running away from him, even now that he's married I still belong to him. He'll kill me."

"Scared?" I ask.

"Oh yes, I keep looking to see if he's on the streets, in case he's outside now, walking around."

"Well, just duck if you see him and I'll go very fast."

Mary has short reddish-brown hair which is thick and curly, a beautiful pale skin and brown eyes. Her accent is unmistakeable Hackney, just as mine has the flat vowels which betray my colonial origin. But my voice has absorbed parts of her past, I remember her hoot of laughter when I first, quite unconsciously, replied, "No it ain't" to a question from her. Just as our voices blend, so have our lives. We three have worked together for over a year. Sally, always more reticent, gives an impression of physical strength which is qualified by sensitive slender hands and a slim body which she hides under chunky sweaters and faded jeans. At one of our weekly workers' meetings Mary announced to our all-woman collective that she had something to tell us. She was very nervous, but it was important for her to chart a change in her life. It was hard for her to start.

"Shall I shut my eyes?" I asked.

"No. It's all right," but there was still a pause.

"Well, I've rehearsed it, and what I want to say is that I've come out as a lesbian and I'm having a relationship with Sally." We hugged and cried. It seemed at that moment that we had formed a new family, replacing the ones we had come from and which had all, to some degree, been withdrawn from us.

Nevertheless we are from different places and I, the most recent arrival in London, have difficulty imagining myself in love with Hackney.

"But what do you miss? This seems just like any part of London. Is it really special to you?"

"Oh, yes. Nowhere else is the same. It's the feel of the pavements under my feet, the shops. Look, there's the Wimpey I used to go to with Sandra, we'd sit there for hours, talking and keeping watch in case Leroy saw us. Some day you must let me take you on a tour. Show you the real Hackney."

"Let's go now. There's time."

"Really, can we go now? Really, really?"

"Why not. Do you want to Sally?" Sally is in the back seat leaning forward, her head between ours. She laughs, "Let's go." Mary is planning where we will go, what she most wants us to see. She is preparing a present for us, an excursion into her past. "Can we get out as well, and walk around? Can we stop the car?"

"Of course. This is your guided tour. Show us the way."

If someone is telling me where to go when I am driving, I lose all sense of direction. The way streets fit together or the ordinary landmarks of a city become less important to me than the voice which is directing me, and I drive as if in a dream. We follow a green articulated lorry as it turns left out of Mare Street. At the end of the road we turn right, then after a while, right again. The streets are becoming narrower and I am conscious only of each intersection and the hazards of each turn. We start driving through run-down estates and single storey brick warehouses.

I have come a long way to be here. I have left a continent, travelled across oceans. The car insulates us from the world outside in which I am a stranger. I listen to Mary's voice as if it is my only link with reality. This journey is not only measured in distance, it is also a journey in time. Mary has spoken to us about the details of her life before we met. Now, because of the one-way system we circle crab-wise around the place where she spent most of her childhood, although we do not know this yet, see only the bare unlovely flats, the treeless streets.

"Look," says Mary, "there's the club I told you about, where I used to go dancing. One of the tenants on the estate asked the Council if he could start a blues club there and they said yes and he played blues music every Saturday night, that's where I met the men who raped me, where I met Leroy too, all the black blokes used to go there." The building is double-storeyed with steel window-frames, an educational air about it. On week-days it is a school for handicapped children.

120

We drive past it and look for a street which will allow us to turn right, but have to avoid the no entry signs and thread a roundabout way through more estates, a wilderness of brick and tar, a few thin trees without spread, no grass. Suddenly Mary asks me to park the car. "Can we get out now?" she asks, holding back her excitement. Sally and I wait outside the car, don't know which way to look, stand on the pavement in the empty street, no shops only square blocks of flats, red brick with windows painted a dirty cream, no balconies.

Mary takes my shoulders in her arm, takes Sally in her other arm, turns us round to face the flats closest to us. "Look!" she says, "The third window up, on the wall in front of you. That was the front room. We used to hang out of the window and yell to anyone passing to get the police when he came. We'd ask them to 'phone the police from that call-box (pointing to a call-box immediately to our left). They knew us at the station, came at once. Sometimes there'd be no-one in the street, and him banging on the door and shouting. He even broke it down once and we locked ourselves in the front room and Bob, my brother, went down out of the window on a sheet. There was no-one in the street, he had to get the police."

"Where was your room?"

"On the other side, come, I'll show you, but first there is something outside I want you to see."

We need to walk round the building as the entrances to the flats are on the other side. The block forms an L round a tarred centre patch with service huts and a wired-in court for football. There is another block opposite which almost completes the square, leaving one side open. Mary leads us to the gate of the wired-in enclosure. She is searching in the tar. "There's something here I want to show you. No, it's gone now. My sister's name in the tar, her husband wrote it. It was here for years". She is still looking. "He wrote Pauline in the tar."

The school I went to was pulled down and rebuilt in another part of the city. Now it is a car-park on the edge of the main shopping centre. My children used to laugh and tease me when I pointed out my old school. I spent four years there. I know how she is feeling.

We don't want to lose momentum, make quickly for the stairway to the flat which is on the far end of the long side.

The stairs are dirty concrete with a smell of damp and urine. We seem to go up and up. Mary is ahead of us, laughing, turning the occasion into an exciting adventure. "Look," she says, "I'll show you the way we used to come home if we'd been out." She leans forward as she climbs, her head peering round each landing, taking two steps at a time, but moving her body stealthily. "He used to wait outside for us to come home, and if we saw him, we'd run."

The shadow of this man lay over Mary's childhood. The man who spent two years in prison for assaulting her mother. "I never called him Dad," says Mary. She has a photograph of her mother pinned up in her front room. It is faded and a little torn, but the woman's face is frank and lovely. "She was beautiful before he broke her jaw."

Now we are standing on the top balcony, Mary points to the right. "The flat is in that corner." With the other hand she shows the path he would have taken, drunk from the pub. "He used to come round there. If we saw him, we'd signal to my auntie, my mother's sister lived in that block of flats opposite, then she could call the police."

"I wish I could get this flat now. I'd give anything to live here. My bedroom was on this side. I'd sit in my window watching for him and playing music on my record player. The kids down on the play-ground used to yell up at me, "Put on a record, Mary!" and I'd put on a reggae record and sit bopping in the window, watching for him at the same time. I'd play the music loud so that they could hear."

We are at the front door. Mary gestures to the two windows on the corridor/balcony. "The bathroom and the kitchen. He broke those. He broke down the door once too."

"Let's knock on the door and ask to see the front room," I suggest. Sally is hesitant, feels it would be an invasion of the lives of the people who live there now, but Mary and I want to go on, further inwards. She looks at me and knocks.

It's no good. First a thin, small man opens the door half-way, he doesn't believe us, is suspicious of our reasons for wanting to enter. Mary says: "I used to live here once, and I wondered if I could show my friends the front room." We know that he must think we are crazy, also want to give him a way out so that he can say no. He disappears inside. A woman opens the door, listens once more to our tale, but this time we are beginning to retreat. "If it is an inconvenience, please don't worry," Sally adds. The woman's face is closed, she mutters something about children asleep, says sorry and we turn away as the lock clicks shut.

As we walk back to the car, Mary says, "I can still remember the number of the telephone box outside, let's see, 254 0798." There are two people in the box, but their bodies don't obscure the number on the 'phone which we can read as we peer in through the glass. "There, you see!" Mary shouts as she reads the number over triumphantly.

This is something tangible, as the front room would have been. This really did happen, this place was hers. She has been away for nine years, the name has gone from the tar in the courtyard, other people live in the flat, but the number is still the same on the public telephone.

"Oh, I'd give anything to get a transfer to this flat, to settle in it with the kids. I was really happy here with Pauline and Bob and Roy and my mom. We knew everyone in the block. When my sister had her kids, they could go down on to the swings and we knew they would be safe. I only moved out when my mom took him back and that was because I couldn't stand the fighting and the fear that he would kill her. I had to leave my job too because I got so tired staying awake all night, waiting up with her for him to come home."

"Where did you go then?"

"I went to Leroy. He was kind to me after the rape and he just seemed to be a friend. I didn't love him, but when he wanted to sleep with me I couldn't refuse because I was grateful to him. And he only beat me after the kids were born."

Sally puts her arm around Mary's shoulders as they wait for me to unlock the car. We are silent as I pull away. I am thinking of where I come from, knowing that it is too far away to share. I wonder how much of our past we can give each other, although we all carry these bundles of memories on our backs, burdens of sentiment. I have wanted to throw away all this extra baggage that I carry around with me, have tried hard to do so. My friendship with Mary has brought me here, to another reality. Today she has given me something important although I am at a loss to say what it is, especially when I view once more the very ordinariness of our surroundings, their dullness. The drab streets overlaid with London dirt.

Of course I can't find my way back, still need the directions until we are once more in Mare Street and making our way through the one-way system to Dalston Junction. I know where I am now, the main roads are familiar to me, it's the local streets, the real neighbourhoods that I become lost in. We drive under a big railway bridge. "This is the bridge where they caught me the night I was raped," says Mary. She was on her way home from the bop with a friend when the car stopped and she was grabbed. The man she was with offered no protection, the others were tougher and there were more than one. I have seen this bridge often, this broad street. It sucks up the emotions of that night as impersonally as the fumes and dust of the city. A girl of fifteen was raped here.

"They were angry with me because I wouldn't dance with them. I said they couldn't just grab me, had to ask properly. No girl had done that to them before. It wasn't because I was white that it happened, it was because I was cheeky. A woman who stood up to them. Afterwards I went straight to the police. Why should they get away with it? But it was terrible in court. I couldn't bear to have my sister and my mother listen to what they had done to me. And then the judge gave them seven years. I know that was because they were black. No white blokes ever get such a long sentence. I do mind about that."

The lights at Dalston Junction are red. "No-one asked us," I mutter as I brake the car. There is no way out of that one except rage.

"Let's go for a drink," suggests Sally. "We can find a pub in Essex Road. I'm hungry as well."

As the weeks pass I become obsessed with that day in Hackney. I see Mary, as I see myself, separated from the past, both of us trying to remake ourselves and our lives, but I am different from her in that I never wish to return. Although the African landscape I have left remains with me, I would not willingly give myself again to the cramped cruelty of colonial life. Nevertheless I still need to be within walking distance of what I was taught from a distance of six thousand miles to believe is the centre of the world. I cannot grasp how anyone would want to live so far away from the lions and fountains in Trafalgar Square, dependent on those slow, rare buses, not even a tube station nearby.

"You were very quiet that day in Hackney," I say to Sally some weeks later.

"It was so real," she replies. "Mary has talked so much about it. I know everything that happened there. And I was scared too. I thought we'd meet him on the stairs, even though I know he's dead."

"It's amazing," I continue, "that Mary still wants to live there now. It's so far from the centre."

"For Mary it is the centre," is Sally's reply.

ABOUT THE AUTHORS

Alison Fell was born in Scotland and educated at rural Scottish schools and at Edinburgh Art College. She has worked in street theatre, women's centres, on *Spare Rib*, as writer-in-residence at a school, and currently at her desk in the new council flat she shares with her son, where she is finishing a novel and wishing she could write a socialist epic poem.

Stef Pixner was born in London in 1945. Has been drawing, writing poetry, songs and stories for most of her life, but has recently left her fulltime job as a lecturer in order to make time to write. Has contributed fiction, reviews and drawings to *Spare Rib*.

Ann Oosthuizen has lived in London since 1973. In 1977 *Spare Rib* published her short story, *Bones*, and at the end of that year she joined the writers group. Since that time, with that support from the group, she has had the nerve to call herself a writer. She translated *The Shame is Over* (1980) by Anja Meulenbelt from the Dutch, for The Women's Press, and is at present busy on a book on sexuality, *For Ourselves*, by the same author, and on a novel.

Tina Reid. I live in London but long for the country where I once lived. My household is large: several adults and children, including my own two. It's hard to conduct a life and to earn a living at the same time as writing, but this is what I aim to do.

Michele Roberts. I was educated at convent school and studied mediaeval literature at Oxford. I'm a Londoner and live near the Portobello Road with three friends. I earn my living as a part-time office worker and book reviewer, and have started writing a third novel.

ABOUT THE GROUP

The authors of this book have met regularly as a group for three years; at times to put books together, this one and our first, self-published collection *Licking the bed clean* (Teeth Imprints, 1978), and continuously to give and get criticism of our current work. The stimulus and friendship of the group has grown to the point where each of us has had the confidence to give up jobs and steady wages in order to write full time. Our work is not collective; we don't write together. The material in this collection was selected by each writer acting on advice from the others. No editorial veto was used. What we do for each other is to give an immediate response to the work, whether it moves and communicates, ideas for solving technical problems, and forthright reactions to contentious material. For us the group has both broken the double isolation of being women and being writers, and also given us the courage to face the necessity of writing alone. It has helped to hold members together through crises of identity/housing/love/work. We're all feminists and also socialists.

Books which include work by the authors

Cutlasses and earrings, edited by Michelene Wandor, Michele Roberts (London: Playbooks, 1976);
Tales I tell my mother, by Zoe Fairbairns et al. (London: Journeyman Press, 1978);
Licking the bed clean, by Alison Fell et al. (London: Teeth Imprints, 1978);
A piece of the night, by Michele Roberts (London: The Women's Press, 1978);
One foot on the mountain, edited by Lilian Mohin (London: Onlywomen Press, 1979);
Hard feelings, edited by Alison Fell (London: The Women's Press, 1979).

About the publishers

Sheba Feminist Publishers registered as a limited co-operative in March, 1980. We are a collective of seven women who meet every Tuesday to make decisions and divide up the work. We had no capital, but we decided to start anyway and use the money we raise from printing books, post-cards and posters to finance the venture. We want to publish fiction, poetry, cartoons, drawings, books of photographs, accessible theory, children's books, books for teenagers — anything that excites us and that we think will be exciting for other women.

Our first act was to bring out our catalogue, listing our first six titles and offering them for mail order in a £10 package. The orders, donations and loans that we have since received have helped us to pay for the stamps and some of our print bills.

Smile Smile Smile Smile is our fourth book. In a sense it is a co-publication, as "Teeth Imprints" had self-published successfully before. Sheba worked closely with the authors in all aspects of the book's production. We hope the book will give you a feel of what care and thought has gone into the production.

Our other titles for 1980 are:

Sour Cream, Jo Nesbitt, Liz Mackie, Lesley Ruda, Christine Roche. A collection of feminist cartoons. 2nd edition. £1.25.

The Ten-Woman Bicycle, Tricia Vita. Illustrations by Marion Crezée. A charming story about how women enter a man's world — together. Particularly suitable for children. £1.25.

Woman and Russia, translated and with an introduction by the Birmingham-based Women and Eastern Europe group. The first feminist samizdat, published in Leningrad in December, 1979 and immediately suppressed. This is its first printing in English. £1.95.

For Ourselves, Anja Meulenbelt/Ariane Amsberg. A radical look at women's sexuality. This book we give ourselves, we hope that women will buy it for themselves and for each other, for their mothers and daughters. We think it will change the way we relate to ourselves and to the other people we make love with. Richly illustrated with photographs and cartoons. £4.50.

The Spare Rib Diary (a co-publication with Spare Rib Magazine). The Spare Rib Diary is already an established Christmas event. Now enlarged with an extended list of information and events and more cartoons and photographs. £2.50.